WITHDRAWN
UTSA LIBRARIES

Reducing Resistance

Methods for Enhancing Openness to Change

Arnold P. Goldstein

Research Press
2612 North Mattis Avenue
Champaign, Illinois 61822
www.researchpress.com

Copyright © 2001 by Arnold P. Goldstein

5 4 3 2 1   01 02 03 04 05

All rights reserved. Printed in the United States of America

Excerpts may be printed in connection with published reviews in periodicals
without express permission. No other part of this book may be reproduced by
any means without the written permission of the publisher.

Copies of this book may be ordered from Research Press at the address given
on the title page.

Cover design by Linda Brown, Positive I.D. Graphic Design
Composition by Jeff Helgesen
Printed by Bang Printing

ISBN 0–87822–469–6
Library of Congress Control Number 2001092368

Library
University of Texas
at San Antonio

To my dear and special Swedish friends,
for their wisdom, energy, and most generous support

Contents

Tables

Preface

A wise publisher with whom I have worked for many years once reflected that many of the best academic and applied books that had been written were, in both style and substance, books that told a story. Often, she added, they contained but a single core idea or theme, and they dealt with it with both curiosity and comprehensiveness. In this book—I hope in a manner reflecting a spirit of energetic inquiry and a measure of comprehensiveness—I seek to tell the story of intervention resistance and its successful management.

It is a hundred-year-long story, one I begin by tracing conceptual origins, evolving definitions over time, and concrete manifestations of intervention resistance in the context of diverse psychotherapies. Over the last century, appraisals of resistance in the therapeutic enterprise have been cast in the form of three contrasting incarnations: resistance as enemy, as interaction, and as myth. As enemy it has been classically viewed as residing in the client, a counterproductive and powerful intrapsychic force to be defeated. As interaction, its roots have been viewed instead as interpersonal, originating from qualities and events in the therapist-client relationship. As myth, it has been seen largely as therapist rationalization for less than competent intervention.

Chapter 1 examines these contrasting views and their respective implications, and provides an array of taxonomies that concretize the manifestations of intervention resistance in the psychotherapeutic arena.

In my view, as both therapy researcher and practitioner, there is little mythical about client resistance. Instead, I believe that both its intrapsychic and interpersonal constructions correctly reflect the realities of the therapist-client discourse. In the book's ensuing chapters, all of which concern ways to reduce resistance, I therefore describe openness-enhancing interventions targeting the client alone and an array of techniques designed to enhance the quality of the therapist-client relationship. Explicitly and by implication, I offer the point that simultaneous use of both approaches constitutes an optimal intervention strategy.

The client may resist therapeutic participation and productive involvement in the change process because of motivational deficits. Chapter 2 takes aim at this domain and explores four routes to motivation enhancement. Commitment may be energized and ambivalence reduced, I hold, by greater attention to an array of client pretreatment characteristics, by employing the techniques of motivational interviewing, by more thorough and skilled goal setting, and via means now available for maximizing the sense of self-efficacy.

As noted, however, client resistance also has its source in the therapeutic relationship, as does the reduction of resistance. Chapter 3 describes intervention techniques designed to enhance the favorability of the therapist-client relationship. In doing so, I draw heavily, by extrapolation, from social-psychological research on the enhancement of interpersonal attraction in nonpsychotherapeutic contexts.

Chapter 4 approaches resistance reduction as a matter of compliance—but in two rather different ways. Research and practice in behavioral medicine speak to compliance as *adherence* to medical regimens. Client, treater, treatment, and contextual variables are each considered, as are parallel means for increasing adherence. In mandated clients, those "sentenced" to psychotherapy, compliance with treatment requirements has been conceptualized more frequently not as voluntary adherence but as involuntary *coercion*. Evidence suggests, perhaps surprisingly, that mandated treatment may indeed be successful, particularly if it reflects such intervention qualities as adequate structure, alliance building, empathy, firmness, and social support.

In contrast to a compliance perspective, chapter 5 focuses on an orienting intervention strategy of client empowerment. I propose that a solution-focused stance—characterized by the combined effects of collaboration, negotiation, appreciation, respect for the client's theory of change, and an emphasis on self-management—may constitute the most effective posture for avoiding and reducing client resistance.

If indeed, as I have stated, client resistance often grows from the therapist-client dyad, just what are the therapist's contributions? Chapter 6 examines the diverse therapist perspectives and behaviors that create or augment client reluctance, reactance, and resistance. Constructive steps the therapist can take in this context are proposed.

Some types of clients are prone to display chronic resistance, and they are particularly challenging intervention targets. I identify and describe several such client types in chapter 6—delinquent, angry, reactant, remote, abrasive, help rejecting, manipulative, and others—and, again, offer suggestions for the management and reduction of the myriad forms of resistance that such clients frequently display.

Inasmuch as intervention resistance is a core dimension of psychotherapy and related interventions, one identified a hundred years ago, the paucity of research on the topic is quite surprising. In the coda that concludes this book, I sketch the key directions I feel research should follow toward greater understanding of resistance's source and influence, as well as describe more successful management of its impact and consequences for openness to change.

CHAPTER 1

Introduction

RESISTANCE AS ENEMY

The concept of resistance as it occurs in the context of psychotherapy was first described by that most creative of psychological practitioners, Sigmund Freud. In *Studies in Hysteria* (Freud, 1895/1955) resistance was portrayed as a "psychological force" directed at preventing unbearable ideas from becoming conscious. It was, in these terms, "an enemy" to be "overpowered," "overcome," "combated," "defeated." In this earliest of conceptual incarnations, resistance was also an ego-protecting force. While operating unconsciously, it served the important purpose of shielding the client from material too unpleasant to contemplate or, at least, regulating and dosing the emergence of such material. Freud had earlier employed suggestion, hypnosis, instructed concentration, and even the laying on of hands (on the patient's temples) as hoped-for means for accessing unconscious material, and he concluded each approach to be inadequate. In the earliest years of the 1900s, he proposed free association for such purposes. Thus, he instructed patients like Dora M. (Freud, 1905/1953) to report whatever came to mind in an unrestrained and uncensored manner. Not infrequently, Dora M. was unable to do so. Instead, she grew silent or superficial or hesitant or in other ways failed to respond as instructed. Clinical experiences such as these progressively led Freud to see the power of patient resistance, its ubiquitousness, its necessity from the patient's perspective and, eventually, the centrality of its management in the therapeutic enterprise.

Strean (1985) describes the dual disclosure-retarding and protective nature of resistance. He comments:

> Although most individuals who enter psychotherapy
> welcome the idea of unburdening themselves and
> saying everything that comes into their minds, sooner

1

or later this process becomes painful and creates anxiety. As clients discuss parts of themselves that have been repressed, confront forbidden sexual and aggressive fantasies, and recover embarrassing memories, they invariably begin to feel guilt and shame. The sense of discomfort can occur in the first, tenth or twentieth session of therapy, but sooner or later all clients feel frightened of what they are revealing. Then they may become silent and evasive, or want to quit the therapy altogether. When clients stop producing material and cease to examine themselves, we refer to this kind of behavior as resistance. Resistance is any action or attitude of the client's that impedes the course of therapeutic work. Inasmuch as every client, to some extent, wants unconsciously to preserve the status quo, all therapy must be carried on in the face of some resistance. (p. 1)

It is clear from such a description of the source, purpose, and pervasiveness of resistance that historically it indeed was viewed as an enemy of therapeutic progress. Furthermore, it was held to be an exclusively intrapsychic enemy. It "resided" in the client—his or her unconscious; its diverse expressions all grew from the client's need to defend and protect. In contrast to later views of resistance as emanating in large part from the patient-therapist interaction, or even from only the therapist, in its earliest conceptualization resistance was viewed as a phenomenon strictly within the client.

Over the span of Freud's career, resistance (along with transference) became a core construct in Freud's development of psychoanalytic theory and treatment. By 1926, Freud (1926/1959) had elaborated the notion into a five-type classification schema. As previously discussed, in the first type of resistance, *repression and other defenses*, to avoid the experience of such painful emotions as shame or guilt, the client blocks awareness from consciousness (i.e., repression), denies that he or she feels anything (i.e., denial), or projects the forbidden sexual or aggressive impulse onto others—the therapist, a spouse, a colleague (i.e., projection). *Transference resistance* assumed particular theoretical importance and therapeutic relevance as Freud's thinking developed: "Analysands wish to perceive the analyst as if he were a figure of the past so that they can avoid facing unpleasant emotions in the present" (Strean, 1985, p. 2). Marshall (1997) describes transference resistance as "the patient recreating the repressed in the therapeutic relationship rather than remembering it" (p. 19). Freud (1926/1959) identified a third type of resistance, *epinosic gain*. Also commonly referred to as secondary gain, an array of disorder-associated benefits— sympathy, concern, attention, reduced responsibility or account-ability, and the like—may be threatened by the therapist's success in moving the client toward "health," and the client may thus resist. In the psychoanalytic schema, this too is an uncon-scious process. Freud's observation that some patients feel quite guilty when they make progress, ostensibly in response to past internalized parental messages, led to his formulation of *super-ego resistance*. The resistance in this instance serves clients' needs for punishment. Finally, Freud referred to the demand for rapid and frequent gratification as *id resistance*. Strean (1995) proposes that

> id resistances are ubiquitous in psychotherapy. Many
> clients want to be the therapist's favorite child and
> make demands on the therapist, such as making con-
> stant phone calls between sessions, pleading for advice
> in and out of sessions, and refusing to accept the frus-
> trations and abstinence that are necessary for therapy to
> have a positive effect. (p. 9)

In addition to these five categories of resistance, Freud (1926/1959) made minor reference to *meta-resistance,* a resist-ance to uncovering and dealing with the other types of resist-ance.

Freud's disciples, and their disciples in turn, have since con-tinued to maintain resistance as a core psychoanalytic con-struct—shaping it, extending its purview, elaborating its meaning, and speculating on its many manifestations and impli-cations. Glover (1928/1955) sought to distinguish between two types of resistance: obvious and unobtrusive or silent. The for-mer includes such behaviors as coming late, missing sessions, prolonged silences, and quitting treatment. The latter, consider-ably more subtle, may be reflected in hyper-politeness, self-criticism, seductiveness, and so forth. Glover also was among the first to associate particular resistances (defenses) with selected clinical syndromes: repression with hysteria, projection with paranoia, reaction formation and undoing with obsessional conditions. Horney (1939) used the term *blockages* to describe the use by clients of evasiveness, argumentativeness, overcompliance, and similar resistive behaviors in the service of preventing repressed material from entering consciousness. Fenichel's (1945) writings on resistance implicitly emphasized the importance of context and content in determining which client behaviors were in fact resistance. Thus, resistance in his view could be manifested by the client's talking too much or too little, focusing too singularly on the past or on the present, or demonstrating change—but only in the consulting room. Fenichel also had much to say about the use, timing, and context of interpretation as means of reducing or resolving client resistances.

Rank (1945) took a very different view of resistance. For him, such behaviors signified autonomy, self-direction, and the patient's "will," and hence he thought they should be taken as signs of therapeutic progress, not otherwise. Such a perspective on the meaning of resistance has, as explained in later chapters, reemerged as part of the therapeutic strategizing of some clinicians today.

Reich's (1933/1951) writings on resistance helped advance earlier notions suggested by Freud to the effect that analysis and resolution of resistance lie at the very core of the goals of psychotherapy. For Reich, resistances manifested in treatment were reflections of "character resistances"—that is, enduring personal traits the client employs to cope with life as he or she perceives it outside the therapy session. Inside and outside the session, such coping often takes the form of heavy reliance on defense mechanisms or, in Reich's terms, "armor" to protect oneself from perceived threats and maintain a psychic status quo. Resistances in therapy, in his view, are manifested less by what clients say and more by how they say it.

Greenson (1967) proposed a multilayered classification schema for describing and categorizing client resistances. Its dimensions are source (id, ego, superego), fixation points (oral, anal, phallic), type of defense used (e.g., repression, regression, projection), diagnostic category (e.g., neurotic depression, hysteria, obsessional neurosis), and ego-alien versus ego-syntonic. Spotnitz (1969) also offered a comprehensive system for categorizing client resistances. As is true for all of the clinicians noted thus far, save perhaps Rank, Spotnitz wrote from a classical psychoanalytic perspective. His categorical system includes the five types of resistance proposed by Freud (1926/1959) and adds (a) treatment destructive resistance, such as missed sessions, lateness, and other behaviors that threaten treatment continuity; (b) inertia resistances, in which, as Marshall (1997) notes, "the patient pleasantly drifts in the analytic current" (p. 33); (c) resistance to analytic progress, a reluctance to explore new emotional territory and the possibility of change; (d) resistance to teamwork and cooperation, in which the focus is on thwarting the development of a growth-enhancing therapist-patient relationship; and (e) termination resistance, a disinclination by the patient to "let go" and function in an autonomous manner. Menninger (1973), Stone (1979), Kaiser (1976), and Fine (1982) are others who have considered resistance and its diverse meanings and manifestations from a psychoanalytic perspective.

This brief parade of the meanings of resistance from early to mid-20th century exemplifies the resistance-as-enemy perspective, in which resistance, variously defined, is in each instance a quality of the client and his or her behavior. As noted at the outset, in this view, resistance resides *within* the client.

Basch (1982) comments in this regard that

> resistance is a much more frustrating phenomenon if we believe on some level that the patient is willfully opposing us and could, if he were only a nicer person and less bent on making our lives miserable, do something about it. However, the way Freud initially described it, resistance is not an interpersonal problem, that is, something that the patient is doing to the therapist, but instead an intrapsychic one that is bringing a struggle within the patient into the foreground of treatment. (p. 4)

RESISTANCE AS INTERACTION

As the century progressed, and as psychotherapy itself moved away from classical psychoanalysis to a more generally interpersonal and object-relations focus, a different perspective on resistance emerged. While not necessarily denying the operation of resistive forces tied to the client's inner dynamics, the interactive view of resistance assumes that aspects of the therapeutic interaction are the primary genesis of client behaviors generally labeled resistance. The client may come late, talk little, avoid depth, be superficial, turn angry, clam up, or quit altogether in response to his or her appraisal that the therapy being offered and the therapy originally sought are simply too discrepant. The discrepancy may be in therapist-client expectations, styles, preferred topics, treatment goals, or other areas. Thus, Kohut (1971) wrote of resistance as a response to the therapeutic process as a whole, rather than as an attempt to hold off awareness of unconscious material. Langs (1981) proposed that many types of client "resistances" are, in his terms, not pathological but appropriate defensive responses to the therapist's errors or improper procedures. He comments that the therapist "is always contributing in some meaningful way to the presence of resistance in the client, and it is incumbent upon the therapist to ascertain his own contribution to each resistance before dealing with those sources which arise primarily from within the patient" (p. 540). Kirmayer (1990) asserts that resistance is often as much a "creation of the therapist's rigidity as it is a feature of the client's interpersonal style" (p. 89). Similar iatrogenic bases for resistance have been noted by Anderson and Stewart (1983), Safran and Muran (2000), and Searles (1977). Cullari (1996) offers a related interactional observation:

> Assuming that the resistance is due primarily to isolated intrapsychic factors detracts us from understanding the client's behavior and from exposing other contributions to the process, including our own role. (p. 3)

> Labeling a client resistive involves a comparison between the ideas or beliefs of the individual and those of the therapist. Thus, a therapist decides that a person would be better off by making changes in a particular direction. If the client does not agree with these proposed changes or is not cooperative, he or she may be labeled resistive. (p. 4)

Cullari notes that the suggestion of some writers (Kris, 1990; Pipes & Davenport, 1990) to solve this definitional dilemma by using the term *resistances* for the unconscious, intrapsychic process within the client and the term *reluctance* for the conscious ambivalence associated with the therapist-patient interaction has not been widely adopted. As Cullari remarks:

The term *resistance,* implying primarily an intrapsychic opposing force in therapy, has probably outlived its usefulness. . . . I propose a view of resistance that focuses on the interactions of the client, the therapist, and the culture at large. Given that psychotherapists are only human and treatment errors are unavoidable, clients are often resistive for justifiable reasons. (1996, p. 6)

Yet when defined in terms of interaction, resistance can not only deter or retard therapeutic progress, it can also serve as an opportunity for gain. Blatt and Erlich (1982) capture the interactive nature of resistance and its change-promoting possibilities:

Resistance, in this expanded psychoanalytic model, can no longer be viewed as an occurrence exclusively within the patient—as a defense against "gaining access to the unconscious"; instead, resistance must be defined in terms of its object relationship—as occurring within the therapeutic dyad, as something between the patient and the therapist that interferes with the flow of the therapeutic process. Conscious and unconscious reluctance, hesitation, fear, inability or unwillingness to consider certain issues may or may not become a resistance depending on the response of the therapist, the capacities of the patient, and the general context of the therapeutic alliance. . . . A therapist can transform this reluctance into a resistance, or respond in a way that enables the patient to gain increased awareness and understanding of his tendencies to limit and/or distort his experiences. (pp. 70–71)

The concept of resistance as an intrapsychic phenomenon has, as I have discussed, a long and prominent history in the annals of psychotherapy, especially psychoanalytic and psychodynamic therapy. Cullari notes, correctly I believe, that this view is based on "dogma, subjective case studies, anecdotal information, or similarly unreliable methods" (1996, p. 3). His inclination is, therefore, largely to reject the intrapsychic meanings of resistance and focus nearly exclusively on its interactional sources and implications. I, too, incline toward this stance but am somewhat less ready to reject the (admittedly "soft") data of the consulting room. So many subsequently empirically validated "facts" of the therapeutic encounter are first noted by reflective clinicians that I resist rejecting (or am reluctant to reject fully) the intrapsychic perspective. The chapters that follow, therefore, concern both the intrapsychic and interactional meanings of resistance.

RESISTANCE AS MYTH

Resistance, in either its intrapsychic or interactive forms, is mostly a child of psychoanalytic psychotherapy. In other approaches, its significance characteristically has been either much diminished or considered irrelevant. Bugental (1987), representing an existential psychotherapeutic perspective, views resistance as serving the purpose of limiting self-disclosure, keeping therapy sessions impersonal, providing the client with an opportunity to preview material before revealing it, maintaining control over the direction and intensity of the therapy sessions, and, as in its traditional explanation of purpose, protecting the client from experience of painful emotions. Although Rogers (1961), from a loosely allied position of humanistic therapy, referred to instigators of client unwillingness to self-disclose, the humanistic perspective's emphasis on the client's striving for growth, awareness, and self-actualization is accompanied by minimal consideration or exploration of resistive influences.

Toward the behavioral end of the psychotherapeutic spectrum, cognitive-behavioral therapists have had a modest amount to say about client resistance; more traditional behavior modification and behavior-analytic therapists, almost nothing at all. In the cognitive-behavioral approach, heavy use is typically made of out-of-session homework assignments. Much of the writing on resistance in the context of this therapeutic approach focuses on failure of the client to understand or execute these assignments. Ellis (1985), reflecting both this focus as well as a locus for resistant behavior in the therapist-client interaction, suggests that resistance may occur when the following are true:

1. Clients do not understand the task assignment.
2. Clients do understand their tasks but do not understand how task completion helps them achieve their therapeutic goals.
3. Clients do understand their tasks but do not believe they are capable of carrying them out.
4. Clients are in fact incapable of executing their tasks.

5. Clients believe they should not have to work in order to change.

6. Therapists fail to prepare their clients adequately for task understanding and completion.

7. Therapists poorly execute their own tasks.

Underlying these manifestations of task-execution resistance are, according to Ellis, fear of discomfort or disclosure, feelings of hopelessness, desire for self-punishment, rebelliousness, secondary gain, various goal-thwarting hidden agendas, resistance to the therapy itself, and an array of dissatisfactions with the therapist or the therapeutic relationship.

Meichenbaum and Gilmore (1982) usefully track the manner in which client resistance may arise, or be minimized, at the referral, initial, intermediate, and termination phases of cognitive-behavioral therapy. As noted earlier is true for Blatt and Erlich (1982), Meichenbaum and Gilmore view resistance as not only progress-retarding blockage but also progress-enhancing opportunity:

> We see the basic key of cognitive-behavioral therapy as training the client to use the scientific model: Identify the working hypothesis, test it empirically, modify it as necessary, and invent new behaviors that will solve problems in a world that works according to the model we hold. . . . "What are the data?" "What is the evidence for my conclusions?" "Are there other explanations?" If the set adopted by the therapist and client is one of a personal scientist, then failures and client resistance, like anomalous data for the scientist, provide additional occasions for examining the nature of the client's cognitions, affects, behaviors, and so on. (p. 38)

In this context of resistance as opportunity and resistance as interaction, Meichenbaum and Gilmore warn practitioners to be especially on guard for what they term *transresistance*—that is, resistance transmitted ping-pong style, back and forth, between therapist and client, client and therapist.

Others working from a cognitive-behavioral perspective take a different view. Rather than viewing resistance as enemy or as interaction, Lazarus and Fay (1982) suggest that the construct resistance is no more than a readily available, blame-avoiding, therapist-constructed myth. Although particular patient disorders may be especially difficult, challenging, and even refractory to change, these observers distinguish between the *problem's* being resistant and the *patient's* being resistant. Furthermore, they purport that

> the concept of "resistance" is probably the most elabo-
> rate rationalization that therapists employ to explain
> their treatment failures. . . . Spoken or unspoken, the
> sentiment is: "It is not my own inadequate assessment
> or faulty diagnosis, nor the limitations of my theories or
> methods, but instead the patient's stubbornness, unwill-
> ingness, or inability to cooperate that accounts for his
> or her lack of progress." . . . The notion that some
> internal process (resistance) is responsible for most or
> many treatment failures or setbacks is simply an unfor-
> tunate though convenient evasion of one's clinical
> responsibilities. (p. 115)

Though it is not my own impression that "resistance as myth" is the predominant view among the psychotherapeutic profes- sions today, Rappaport (1997) holds otherwise. He asserts, in fact, that "the overwhelmingly popular view of resistance among theoreticians is that it is largely a problem of therapist perception or countertransference" (p. 2).

Yet another view of resistance has predominated among those promoting a behavior modification approach to psycho- logical intervention. Rather than seeing resistance as an intrapsy- chic phenomenon operating in the client, a process operating within the therapist-client interaction, or a rationalization pro- moted by blame-avoiding therapists, the behavior modification movement early on treated resistance as a nonissue. Clients were viewed as rationally complying with therapeutic instructions (Goldfried, 1982). There were exceptions to this prevailing view, however. Weinberg and Zaslove (1963) reported three types of resistance in systematic desensitization. Direct resistance mani- fested in restlessness, boredom, or uncooperativeness. Indirect resistance was overtly reflected in coming late for sessions, not following treatment rules, or failing to execute assigned home- work. Resistance associated with the intervention setting was concretized by efforts to please the therapist or apparent lack of motivation. Other, spotty references to resistance in the context of behavior modification have come from D'Alessio (1968), Davison (1973), and Kanfer and Schefft (1988). Most, however, have seemed to agree with Sundel (1982) that there is little to gain by recognizing and employing the construct. Perhaps, however, reflected here is theoretical preference rather than clinical reality. As Wachtel (1982) asserts:

> In the behavioral literature, references to resistance are scant. If one only *reads* about behavior therapy, one is likely to conclude either that behavior therapists do not understand or do not notice resistance or that their methods overcome resistance or make it irrelevant. Such an illusion is likely to disappear quite rapidly if one sits down face to face with a behavior therapist and gets to talking cases. (p. xiv)

Resistant Behaviors: Categories and Typologies

The preceding pages have been a brief tour of the status and meaning of resistance through time and across psychotherapeutic approaches. Like so much that is true of psychotherapy, differences in interpretation are often much more apparent than real. The diverse perspectives reflected in theoretical writings seem to blend into much greater similarity in the reality of the therapeutic session. However the phenomenon of resistance is construed, all therapists experience and must deal with client behaviors that at best stall, and at worst thwart, the positive goals of the intervention.

The present section concerns the specific client behaviors that concretize, constitute, and express resistance. Lists of such behaviors in the literature are several; their differences are few. The following discussion therefore covers a representative sample of the categories and typologies of resistive behavior that have been offered in the context of various psychotherapies.

Blatt and Erlich (1982) offer the following categories:

1. *Episodic resistance:* A delimited or circumscribed defense or reluctance focused on a specific conflictual issue that is evident for one or a few sessions.

2. *Transference resistance:* A repetitive reenactment of earlier expressions of interpersonal relating. As the authors note, "Transference in and of itself is a form of resistance because

it reflects the reluctance or inability to relinquish well-established, deeply ingrained, repetitive modes of adaptation in favor of attempting new, alternative, and more mature modes" (p. 73).

3. *Developmental resistance:* A resistance to change, growth, and gain, and a holding on to the psychic status quo and one's dysfunctional "adjustment."

Patterson (1982) writes of two comprehensive levels of treatment resistance. Microlevel resistance is exemplified by client challenges, disagreements, and other negative verbal responses to therapeutic influence. Macrolevel resistance, less subtly, is indicated by failure to complete homework assignments, failure to show up for sessions, or dropping out of treatment altogether.

Munjack and Oziel (1978) propose a five-category system. In Type I resistance the client simply fails to understand what the therapist wants or expects. Responsible here, Kottler (1991) suggests, may be the client's lack of sophistication and naivete, inadequate or incomplete communication by the therapist regarding the core tasks of the therapy, or a combination of such factors. In Type II resistance the client may understand the tasks to be accomplished but lacks the skills to complete them. Low expectations for success and inadequate motivation to change characterize Type III resistance. Apathy and indifference are among its chief features. Type IV resistance is resistance in the classical psychoanalytic use of the term. As Kottler describes it, "The client starts to back off as repressed feelings begin to surface. Work can be proceeding smoothly and consistently until a nerve is struck and then . . . the client does everything possible to sabotage further progress" (p. 10). Finally, Type V resistance reflects secondary gains, which clients may be accorded as a result of their disorder and its overt symptoms.

Miller and Rollnick (1991), in the context of their motivational interviewing approach (see chapter 2), offer the resistance classification schema shown in Table 1.1. Otani (1989) proposes a comprehensive schema consisting of diverse forms of client resistance assigned to the four broad categories shown in Table 1.2. One category system helpfully organizes the resistances that may emerge as a function of stage of therapy

TABLE 1.1
Categories of Client Resistance Behavior

1. Arguing: The client contests the accuracy, expertise, or integrity of the therapist.

   1a. *Challenging.* The client directly challenges the accuracy of what the therapist has said.

   1b. *Discounting.* The client questions the therapist's personal authority and expertise.

   1c. *Hostility.* The client expresses direct hostility toward the therapist.

2. Interrupting: The client breaks in and interrupts the therapist in a defensive manner.

   2a. *Talking over.* The client speaks while the therapist is still talking, without waiting for an appropriate pause or silence.

   2b. *Cutting off.* The client breaks in with words obviously intended to cut the therapist off (e.g., "Now wait a minute. I've heard about enough").

3. Denying: The client expresses an unwillingness to recognize problems, cooperate, accept responsibility, or take advice.

   3a. *Blaming.* The client blames other people for problems.

   3b. *Disagreeing.* The client disagrees with a suggestion that the therapist has made, offering no constructive alternative. This includes the familiar "Yes, but . . . ," which explains what is wrong with suggestions that are made.

   3c. *Excusing.* The client makes excuses for his or her own behavior.

   3d. *Claiming impunity.* The client claims that he or she is not in any danger (e.g., from drinking).

   3e. *Minimizing.* The client suggests that the therapist is exaggerating risks or dangers and that it "really isn't so bad."

   3f. *Pessimism.* The client makes general statements about self or others that are pessimistic, defeatist, or negativistic in tone.

   3g. *Reluctance.* The client expresses reservations and reluctance about information or advice given.

   3h. *Unwillingness to change.* The client expresses a lack of desire or an unwillingness to change, or an intention not to change.

TABLE 1.1 *(continued)*

4. Ignoring. The client shows evidence of not following or ignoring the therapist.

   4a. *Inattention.* The client's response indicates that he or she has not been following or attending to the therapist.

   4b. *Nonanswer.* In answering a therapist's query, the client gives a response that is not an answer to the question.

   4c. *No response.* The client gives no audible or nonverbal reply to a therapist's query.

   4d. *Sidetracking.* The client changes the direction of the conversation that the therapist has been pursuing.

Note. From *Motivational Interviewing: Preparing People to Change Addictive Behavior* (p. 103) by W. R. Miller and S. Rollnick, 1991, New York: Guilford. Reprinted by permission. (Based on information reported in "Observation of Client Resistance" by P. Chamberlain, G. Patterson, J. Reid, K. Kavanagh, & M. Forgatch, 1984, *Behavior Therapy, 15*, pp. 144–155.)

(Beitman & Yue, 1999). Construing a four-stage sequence, they propose the stage-by-type-of-resistance schema outlined in Table 1.3. Higgs (1992) has proposed a similar view of client resistance changing in form as treatment unfolds. In this instance, the treatment involved is group psychotherapy, and the stages demarcated are initial distrust, transition, working, and termination.

Though few clinicians or investigators explicitly make the point, it is of considerable importance to note in connection with resistance category systems that, whereas manifestations of resistance may reflect the same client affect or intent, any given resistive behavior can also reflect multiple underlying causes. As an example of the latter, Harris and Watkins (1987) observe that clients may elect to remain silent because (a) they resent being forced into treatment and are exercising the only means of control available to them; (b) they do not understand what they are supposed to do or say, so they choose to say nothing; (c) they assume no personal responsibility for their presenting concerns, and thus it is someone else, not they, who should be speaking; or (d) they fear the therapist may breach confidentiality and reveal information to a third party.

Resistance categorizations follow not only from clinician preferences (e.g., intrapsychic or interactive) but also from the

---

TABLE 1.2
Four Categories of Client Resistance

   I. Quantity resistance (withholding communication)
      1. Being silent
      2. Making infrequent responses
      3. Making minimal responses
      4. Engaging in incessant rambling
  II. Response-content resistance (restricting content)
      5. Making small talk
      6. Intellectualizing
      7. Asking rhetorical questions
      8. Engaging in obsessive rambling
 III. Response-style resistance (being manipulative)
      9. Discounting
     10. Being seductive
     11. Externalizing
     12. Forgetting
  IV. Logistic management resistance (violating rules)
     13. Missing appointments
     14. Delaying payment
     15. Making improper requests
     16. Displaying inappropriate behavior

Note. Reprinted from A. Otani, "Client Resistance in Counseling: Its Theoretical Rationale and Taxonomic Classification," *Journal of Counseling and Development, 67,* 1989, page 460. © ACA. Reprinted with permission. No further reproduction authorized without written permission of the American Counseling Association.

nature of the psychotherapeutic approach. Although there are numerous obvious commonalities regarding what constitutes resistance across therapies (e.g., silence, quitting), there also appear to be therapy-specific resistances. In the context of family therapy, for example, Andersen and Stewart (1983) specify initial (pretreatment and early treatment) resistances, those associated with the therapeutic contract, challenges to the therapist's competence, resistance produced by helping systems, and resistance common to the ongoing family treatment itself. With a similar family focus, Solomon (1974) identifies resistances to the therapy and the therapist-family interaction, and what he terms "family-specific resistances." Among the latter are scapegoating, keeping family secrets, denying other family members' evident

---

TABLE 1.3
Forms of Resistance at Different Stages of Psychotherapy

Engagement	Resist the establishment of the working alliance, by, for instance:
	• Failing to appear for an appointment
	• Criticizing the therapist's age, sex, inexperience, training, race and/or religion
Pattern search	Fail to report information relevant to defining the patterns, as seen in:
	• Excessive silence
	• Withholding important information
	• Talking about subjects irrelevant to pattern definition
	• Refusing to do role-playing and/or homework
Change	Fail to generate alternatives:
	• Agree to initiate a new pattern but fail to do so
	• Refuse to comply with the therapist's suggestions
Termination	Fail to terminate therapy, such as:
	• Continue to call the therapist or go to see the therapist without appointment after termination
	• Believe that the therapist must be available for effective decision making

---

Note. From LEARNING PSYCHOTHERAPY (p. 226) by Bernard D. Beitman and Dongmei Yue. Copyright © 1999 by Bernard D. Beitman, M.D., and Dongmei Yue, M.D. Used by permission of W. W. Norton & Company, Inc.

emotion, protecting or joining other members' resistance, accusing others of disloyalty to prevent disclosures, and threatening to desert the family as change approaches. Framo (1965) has also offered a family therapy–oriented resistance classification schema.

Luther and Loev (1981) have provided a similarly useful typology of participant resistance in marital therapy. It includes (a) *individual resistances,* such as seeking to serve as co-therapist, spouse blaming, concealing of feelings, or denying apparent change in one's spouse; (b) *collusive resistances,* including both partners' withholding secrets, focusing on topics other than the marital relationship, and agreeing to terminate the therapy prematurely; and (c) *therapist-inspired resistances,* such as allying with one spouse against the other or accepting the role of secret bearer when becoming privy to information the other spouse does not know.

Finally, in group psychotherapy, as in the family and marital therapies, there are both individual member resistances and systemic (in this case, group) resistances. Individually, Yalom (1970)—in his description of "problem patients"—identifies five types of individuals whose diverse behaviors each in their own way seek to thwart the group psychotherapeutic process. The *monopolist* fills the briefest silence, responds to every statement in the group, and often seems to chatter on without end. The *help-rejecting complainer* repeatedly requests help in direct and indirect ways from the group and then, when it is offered, rejects it. As Yalom notes, this type of client seems to take pride in the insolubility of his or her problems. A third type of resistive group member is the *self-righteous moralist.* Central here is an unremitting need to be right and to prove others wrong, especially when one or another moral issue is involved. The *doctor's assistant* repeatedly offers advice to other group members, often in the form of platitudes, and simultaneously resists admitting personal weaknesses or needs of his or her own. And finally, as in all forms of therapy, there is the *silent patient.* The basis for nonparticipation may be any one of a number of reasons, but this patient passively, quietly, and silently plays out a distanced role in the therapy group.

At the systemic (group or subgroup) level, resistance may take form as clique formation or fractionalization, leading to inclusion-exclusion problems, subgroup conflict, lowered group cohesiveness, rivalries, and premature termination (Yalom, 1970). Nitsun (1996) also adds mistrust in and of the group, leading to clashes between members as well as overt accusations that the group is "second best" treatment, that it gives too little time per person, and that other members and their problems are a liability.

Also at the systemic level, in this instance regarding therapeutic groups whose members are delinquent adolescents, Redl and Wineman (1957) write of "escape into love," in which group members promote a loving relationship with the group therapist but continue their delinquency unabated outside the group. The group may also engage in "protective provocation," whereby members deliberately elicit the therapist's rejection to avoid meaningful treatment.

EMPIRICAL FINDINGS ON RESISTANCE

This introduction to the topic of resistance rests almost entirely on a foundation of clinical theory, clinical lore, practitioner impression, consulting room experience, case study, and therapeutic anecdote. Facts about resistance are few. The little empirical information that does exist seems a fitting conclusion to this stage-setting opening chapter. According to Chamberlain, Patterson, Reid, Kavanagh, and Forgatch (1984), resistance tends to be lowest at the beginning and end of therapy, and highest in the middle stages. As might be expected, given their theoretical predilections, when given the same case materials, psychoanalytic therapists perceive more client resistance than do behavior modification therapists (Verhulst & van de Vijer, 1990).

Regarding the grand resistance of whether the client shows up at all, studies of "pre-intake attrition" report that between a quarter (Larsen, Nguyen, Green, & Attkisson, 1983) and a half (Phillips & Fagan, 1982) of prospective clients fail to keep their first appointment, with men being more likely than women to do so (Hafner, 1983). When asked why they missed their first appointment, men's explanations were (in order of frequency) did not know why, forgot, condition improved, and had anxiety about participation (Noonan, 1973).

Several dozen studies of premature termination have been conducted across a wide variety of client types, disorders, and therapeutic approaches. Generally, the finding is that 30 to 60 percent of all patients are gone after but a session or two (Baekeland & Lundwall, 1975; Garfield, 1994). As suggested earlier in this chapter, however, at times client resistance lies more in the eyes of the therapist than in the actual behavior or affect of the client. "Premature" termination, for many individuals, may not be premature at all. I have suggested elsewhere (Goldstein, 1962) that the intake interview and pretreatment diagnostic testing may be construed and experienced as therapy by the client, yielding a process I term "unspontaneous remission," an enhanced belief of likely positive outcome ("If they are taking me as a client, my condition must be treatable") and consequently reduced anxiety. Bloom (1981) has, in fact, reported such intake-session consequences in about 70 percent of clients queried. Pekarik (1985) adds relevantly that clients' expectations about optimal treatment length are, characteristically, considerably shorter than those held by the therapist. In brief, so-called premature termination of treatment for many clients reflects not resistance but, instead, appropriate and optimal length. Whether "early" termination is appropriate and optimal or premature and therefore resistive, therapists have had some reasonable success in moderating departure from therapy by cueing the client (letter or telephone prompts about one's appointments), reducing perceived barriers (automatically setting appointments, ensuring brief delay between intake and first session), or seeking to increase motivation (e.g., through contracting; Macharia, Leon, Rowe, Stephenson, & Haynes, 1992).

For those for whom the leaving is premature (i.e., psychological help is needed but declined) reasons given for termination include the stigma of seeing a therapist; difficulty acknowledging they have a problem or need help; fear of embarrassment, of change, or of finding out they have a severe disorder; fear that their symptoms will get worse if explored in therapy; fear that therapy will bring back traumatic memories; fear of being asked to engage in anxiety-arousing behaviors; and the belief that there is little or no hope for change (Cullari, 1996; Garfield, 1994; Kushner & Sher, 1991; Munjack & Oziel, 1978). Of the very many client characteristics examined as possible predictors of what Reis and Brown (1999) wisely label "unilateral [rather than premature] termination" only client socioeconomic status and ethnicity reliably do so. More significant in leading to staying or going, it appears, are dynamic qualities of the therapist-patient interaction—shared expectations, reciprocal likability, the quality of the initial working alliance. Mohl, Martinez, Ticknor, Huang, and Cordell (1991) found that unilateral terminators like their clinicians less, feel less well-liked and less respected by them, and experience a weaker alliance. Garfield (1994); Mennicke, Lent, and Burgoyne (1988); and several other investigators report a similar association for unconfirmed client expectations.

CONCLUSIONS

I have sketched in this chapter the history of the concept of resistance; noted that over time it has been viewed as enemy, as interaction, or as a convenient myth; and sampled a number of the resistance category systems that have been proposed. The chapters that follow concern this book's main theme, resistance reduction. In turn, I will present and examine the primary means currently available for this purpose: motivation enhancement (chapter 2), relationship enhancement (chapter 3), compliance techniques (chapter 4), and client empowerment (chapter 5). The discussion concludes (save the coda) with a consideration in chapter 6 of the role of therapist counterresistance in client resistance and of the particularly challenging nature of an array of client characteristics.

CHAPTER 2

Motivation Enhancement

Opportunities for the enhancement of client motivation to minimize client resistance begin before treatment begins. In a seminal paper titled "Precursors of Change: Pivotal Points of Involvement and Resistance in Psychotherapy," Hanna (1996) draws attention to client qualities existing prior to treatment that appear to be prerequisites for adequate levels of motivation and involvement—regardless of the psychotherapeutic approach. Their absence or inadequacy is the soil in which resistance takes root and grows. Specifically, these precursors are a sense of necessity, willingness to experience anxiety, awareness of the problem, problem confrontation, effort, hope, and social support. When these qualities are in place, holds Hanna, therapeutic progress and change are likely. When they are deficient or absent, client resistance will be apparent and change retarded. As he puts it, "These client variables may be seen as pivots, or hinges upon which change and resistance hang like a door that swings open or closed as the case may be" (p. 231).

PRECURSORS OF CHANGE

A sense of necessity is a sense of urgency or need for some form of change, and it is important for this urgency to occur sooner rather than later. In the absence of a sense of necessity, Hanna suggests, clients will tend to be inattentive, lackadaisical, and apathetic. In addition, they are likely to procrastinate about completing homework assignments, come late for sessions, or miss sessions altogether. A sense of necessity may be enhanced by pointing out to clients the discrepancies between the consequences of their current behavior and the consequences associated with their significant life goals.

Willingness to experience anxiety is the second proposed precursor. It is defined as a readiness to undergo the emotions and anxieties that are inevitable if one is open to the change process. As Hanna notes, it is the opposite of defensiveness, defined as an attempt to avoid anxiety. Clients unwilling to experience necessary turmoil will behave in a remote and detached manner during therapy sessions and tend to be evasive, elusive, intellectualizing, and so forth. They may also be prone to miss or come late for sessions, not because they have little sense of their importance or urgency, but as a means of avoiding anxiety. Hanna proposes a number of means for promoting this precursor, including gradual exposure, imagery targeted to anxiety-arousing situations, and "no pain, no gain" types of cognitive reframing.

Awareness of the problem is the client's ability to identify the concerns—interpersonal, affective, cognitive, behavioral—that must be addressed and are central to the therapy. Such awareness involves reorganizing problems to be dealt with as well as understanding their underlying contributing factors. Awareness is, Hanna suggests, the opposite of denial. A lack or deficiency in such awareness may be manifested in such resistant behaviors as vagueness and uncertainty, denial that an (obvious) problem exists (or at least consistently minimizing its importance), and a repeated tendency to assign to others the responsibility for one's problems. Self-monitoring, paradoxical intervention, role-playing persons who know the client well, the empty chair technique, and Beck's (1976) distancing technique may be used fruitfully to enhance problem awareness.

Problem confrontation involves actions taken by the client to look more deeply into his or her problems and their bases. In contrast to problem awareness, which is more contemplative and passive, problem confrontation is a more active taking on, encountering, facing up. Hanna describes it as "continuing to examine or investigate—digging in one's heels for sustained observation in spite of tendencies toward avoidance or acting out" (p. 238). Hesitancy to explore, minimizing excuses, circumlocution, and balking at the magnitude of a problem are among the resistances that are reciprocal to confronting the problem. Self-monitoring and gradual exposure techniques are the main clinical interventions relevant in this context.

The fifth precursor is *effort,* the deliberate exertion by the client of mental or physical energy toward therapeutic tasks and goals. Effort can be as simple as attending to what the therapist has to say or as complex as carrying out a series of challenging homework assignments. Clients lacking the willingness or ability to invest such effort will procrastinate around therapy demands, give up easily if they are undertaken, and more generally devote only limited energy to the psychotherapeutic endeavor. Interventions to enhance effort include cognitive restructuring and mental imagery techniques.

Hope is the expectation that matters will change for the better. Hope as a precursor to motivation for psychotherapy is examined in Frank's (1991) exploration of the role of client demoralization as it influences treatment course and outcome. As relevant to client motivation and resistance, Hanna asserts that the hopeful person sees therapy as a tool and an opportunity for a better future. A general sense of confidence and anticipation of goal attainment are the markers for hope. Contrariwise, low levels of hopefulness are marked by pessimism, little problem-solving confidence, easy discouragement, cynicism, and even despair. Generating and rehearsing options, examining habitual expectations, and problem-solving training or other procedures for improving self-efficacy are hope-building interventions.

Social support, the final precursor, is the interpersonal network in which one is embedded and the psychological and material aid available therefrom. It is concretized by the helpful, useful, affirming, and facilitative relationships one has with family, friends, colleagues, and others. Low motivation is promoted by lack of social support, abuse, ridicule, disparagement, or indifference. Hanna recommends social skills training, assertiveness training, and interpersonal approaches to the treatment itself as remedial. Hanna aptly concludes that his explication of these seven precursors is an

> attempt to help clients achieve change more quickly through diminished resistance. Hypothetically, if resistance were removed from the equation, therapeutic change would take place quicker, smoother, deeper, and with a more global effect. Recognizing and utilizing the precursors can be seen as an attempt to move therapy conditions toward ideal by establishing the proper circumstances that reduce resistance and cultivate change. (1996, p. 259)

Prochaska, DiClemente, and Norcross's (1992) "stages of change" model of a client's psychotherapeutic career is an umbrella under which Hanna's precursor interventions may be implemented—especially as concerns their selection and timing. Prochaska et al. propose that psychotherapeutic involvement passes through five stages: precontemplation, contemplation, determination, action implementation, and maintenance. The first two are pretherapeutic stages and thus constitute prime occasions for attention to precursor enhancement. Prochaska et al. add further means to maximize client motivation during the pretherapy period. During precontemplation, the individual—by definition—is not considering becoming a client. Four types of precontemplators are proposed. Reluctant precontemplators are those who, through lack of information or inertia, do not want to consider change. They are more reluctant than resistant, and may decide (i.e., be motivated to) enter psychotherapy if provided with relevant information in a sensitive way. Rebellious precontemplators, in contrast, are motivated, but in their case it is motivation to avoid therapy. They are heavily invested in maintaining the status quo, in not altering their problem behavior, and will actively resist efforts to change them. Providing them with choices and using paradoxical interventions are helpful in this case. The resigned precontemplator has more or less given up. Past change attempts may have been undertaken and failed. Resigned precontemplators present a pattern of demoralization, lack of energy, and minimal expectations for change. Prochaska et al. propose as useful exploring barriers to change with the client, as well as instituting any procedures (e.g., incremental exposure or participant modeling) that have the potential to augment self-efficacy and instill hope. DiClemente et al. (1991) describe the final type of precontemplator as follows:

> The rationalizing precontemplator has all the answers where the resigned precontemplator has none. These clients are not considering change because they have figured out the odds of personal risk, or they have plenty of reasons why the problem is not a problem or is a problem for others but not for them. . . . The key to identifying this type of client occurs when the interview begins to feel like a debate or a session of point-counterpoint. Empathy and reflective listening seem to work best with this type of client. (pp. 295–296)

Whether clients are reluctant, rebellious, resigned, or rationalizing, Prochaska et al.'s (1992) attention to the enhancement of motivation at the precontemplation stage, in combination with Hanna's (1996) focus on maximizing precursors, carries the significant meta-message that efforts to reduce resistance can and should commence as early as possible, even before the therapy begins.

As the client-to-be more seriously considers the possibility of change, of entering psychotherapy, his or her thinking is typically marred by considerable ambivalence. He or she has thus entered Prochaska et al.'s (1992) contemplation stage. To change ambivalent contemplation into a commitment, Prochaska et al. recommend the strategies and techniques of motivational interviewing (Miller & Rollnick, 1991), next discussed.

MOTIVATIONAL INTERVIEWING

Especially relevant during the contemplation stage but at times necessary across the entire psychotherapeutic process, motivational interviewing is conceptualized as a set of procedures the therapist implements to reduce ambivalence. As Miller and Rollnick remark:

> Motivation becomes an important part of the counselor's task. It is the counselor's responsibility not only to dispense advice, but to motivate—to increase the likelihood that the client will follow a recommended course of action toward change. From this perspective, it is no longer sensible for a therapist to blame a client for being unmotivated to change, any more than a salesperson would blame a potential customer for being unmotivated to buy. Motivation is an inherent and central part of the professional's task. (1991, p. 19)

The stage is set for motivational interviewing, and its companion goals of increasing motivation and commitment and reducing ambivalence and resistance, by attending to such matters as removing barriers to participation (cost, transportation, child care, waiting time); increasing the client's sense of choice (regarding methods of approach, treatment goals); decreasing the desirability of inappropriate behaviors (emphasizing awareness of adverse consequences, changing enabling social contingencies); providing ongoing feedback (regarding personal and social costs and benefits); progressively clarifying treatment goals; and offering help to the client in an active and forthright manner (e.g., a telephone call or handwritten note regarding the next appointment). Goal setting is discussed in more detail in the following section.

With such strategic positions as their stance, Miller and Rollnick describe the specific procedures that do (and do not) constitute the motivational interviewing approach. First, and most important, the approach eschews persuasion. When the client's ambivalence is seen as something to be overcome by educating the client about the need for commitment, the following counterproductive sequence is likely to ensue:

> The counselor attempts to persuade the client that the problem is serious and must be changed. This represents one side of the conflict from which the person already suffers, and the client's response is almost completely predictable. Faced with the "You should change" side of the conflict, the client gives voice to the other side: "Yes, but . . ." This signals something for the counselor: "Aha! This client is in denial." If the counselor therefore escalates by arguing more "persuasively," the client counters with still stronger reasons why the behavior is attractive or acceptable, the problem "isn't that serious," and change is not required. . . . They are, in essence, acting out the client's conflict. (1991, p. 37)

Motivational interviewing, in contrast, deals with client ambivalence by operationalizing five intervention principles. The first is to *express empathy*. I will have considerably more to say regarding therapist empathy as it bears upon resistance management and reduction in chapter 3, on the therapist-client relationship. Empathy is, indeed, a significant component of this relationship and accordingly has a prominent place in motivational interviewing. As its developers have suggested, "Through skillful reflective listening, the therapist seeks to understand the client's feelings and perspectives without judging, criticizing, or blaming" (p. 55). Accepting clients as they are, ambivalence regarding change and all, frees them to change, whereas insistence on change, perhaps via a process of reactance, yields heightened defensiveness (Goldstein & Michaels, 1985).

The second operating tactic at the heart of motivational interviewing is to *develop discrepancy*. The therapist gently but steadfastly creates and amplifies in the client's mind a discrepancy between the costs of his or her current behaviors and benefits of more long-term personal goals. In essence, the task is one of creating cognitive dissonance. The third operating theme of this approach is to *avoid argumentation*. Confrontation is "soft"; accusation and argumentation are avoided. The therapist, therefore, *rolls with resistance,* the fourth feature of motivational interviewing. Client statements are reframed to create momentum toward change and away from ambivalence. Ambivalence is openly acknowledged as natural and expected. The final recommendation, elaborated at greater length later in this chapter, is to *support self-efficacy.* Nothing motivates better than task success. Subsequent discussion concerns existing means for enhancing clients' sense that they indeed possess the abilities necessary to bring about positive therapeutic change.

These core tactics find expression in motivational interviewing in the generous use of open-ended questions; reflective listening to affirm client effort; and, especially, therapist attempts to elicit, support, and encourage self-motivational statements by the client. These statements are of four types. The first is *problem recognition*—for example, "I never realized how much I am drinking" and "I guess there's more of a problem here than I thought." The second is *expression of concern,* such as "I'm really worried about this" or "I feel pretty hopeless." *Intention to change* is the third category. Examples include "I've got to do something to feel better" and "I think the time has come to stop drinking." Finally, such statements may express *optimism* and certainly are to be encouraged—for instance, "I think I can do it" and "Now that I've decided, I'm sure I can change."

Motivational interviewing appears to be a particularly promising approach to dealing with the ambivalence that underlies much of what makes up client resistance in psychotherapy. Further investigation of the factors identified by Miller and Rollnick (1991) is well worth undertaking.

GOAL SETTING

In its focus thus far on processes of change, the precontemplation and contemplation stages of treatment, and motivational interviewing, this chapter has concerned client resistance and its management prior to and at the beginning of treatment. A highly relevant concern during this time frame is client goal setting.

Goals are "thoughts about desired or undesired states or outcomes that one would like to achieve or avoid" (Ford, 1992, p. 43). Locke and Latham (1990) use "goals" generically to subsume meanings of intention, purpose, aim, end, and objective. Others have represented goals as "current concerns" (Klinger, 1975), "personal strivings" (Emmons, 1993), "personal projects" (Little, 1983), "life task[s]" (Cantor & Langston, 1989), and "possible selves" (Markus & Nurius, 1986). Ford and Nichols (1987) have developed the comprehensive taxonomy of human goals presented in Table 2.1.

Goals vary both in content and intensity. Content refers to the result or object being sought. Intensity refers to the goal's importance in the person's hierarchy of goals, the effort required to reach it, and the degree to which the person is committed to it. Goal selection and attainment are influenced by a number of factors, of which an important one is the individual's perceived self-efficacy (see the next section in this chapter). Self-efficacy, as Locke and Latham (1990) have suggested, affects goal choice, goal commitment, and response to goal-relevant feedback. A number of alternative goal characteristics appear to make goal attainment more or less likely to occur. Chief among these influences are difficulty and clarity or specificity. A comprehensive review of goal attainment research across a wide range of tasks, settings, subjects, criteria, and time spans led Locke and Latham to conclude that "nearly 400 (mostly experimental) studies have shown that specific, difficult goals lead to better performance than specific, easy goals, vague goals such as 'do your best,' or no goals" (1990, p. 240).

Proximal goals generally appear to facilitate performance more than do longer term goals, although, as Ford (1992) counsels, "effective functioning requires a strategic emphasis on attainable short-term goals combined with a periodic review of the long-term goals that give meaning and organization to one's short-term pursuits" (p. 99).

Most research comparing self-set (or participative) goal setting with goals imposed by others does not show goal attainment superiority for participative goal setting. Satisfaction is often higher, but performance is not.

Perhaps once a goal is imposed and accepted sufficiently for task performance to commence, "ownership" in fact shifts, and the goal becomes one's own. Further, what may be central for performance is, once again, one's perceived self-efficacy vis-à-vis the self- or other-imposed goal, rather than the source of the goal's imposition. Locke and Latham have observed:

> Contrary to the conventional wisdom that letting people have a say or make choices leads to greater feelings of self-control or commitment and hereby better perform-ance, it may be that telling people what goals to try for is in itself an indirect means of inducing self-efficacy, especially when the goals are high. . . . The assignment of a specific goal . . . implies that the person is capable of achieving the goal. (1990, p. 90)

Commitment and adherence to goal attainment is highly related to actual performance. Such commitment may be height-ened by peer influences, the degree to which performance is pub-lic, one's commitment, and the level of incentive or reward associated with the goal. When the goal is imposed or assigned by others, commitment will be heightened when the goal-assigning person or persons are trustworthy, supportive, and knowledge-able in goal-relevant domains; provide an understandable ration-ale for goal striving; imply opportunities for self-development; and are physically present during task activities.

Motivation for goal attainment connects to actual perform-ance outcomes by regulating certain aspects of goal-oriented behavior—specifically, the intensity of effort the individual expends in goal striving, the duration or persistence of such effort, and the choices the person makes to channel attention and action in the direction of goal achievement. The observation that people favor difficult, specific goals is largely an observation of effort: People work harder for clear, difficult (but attainable) goals. Persistence is effort maintained over time. As with effort or intensity, a number of investigations have shown that specific, challenging goals lead people to work longer at a variety of tasks than do other types of goals. The last aspect of goal striving is behavior direction. Goals orient the person toward relevant activ-ities and materials and away from irrelevant ones. They also affect how goal-relevant information is processed by activating particular stored knowledge and skills that may be useful for

TABLE 2.1
Ford and Nichols Taxonomy of Human Goals

DESIRED WITHIN-PERSON CONSEQUENCES

Affective Goals

Entertainment — Experiencing excitement or heightened arousal; avoiding boredom or stressful inactivity

Tranquility — Feeling relaxed and at ease; avoiding stressful overarousal

Happiness — Experiencing feelings of joy, satisfaction, or well-being; avoiding feelings of emotional distress or dissatisfaction

Bodily Sensations — Experiencing pleasure associated with physical sensations, physical movement, or bodily contact; avoiding unpleasant or uncomfortable bodily sensations

Physical Well-Being — Feeling healthy, energetic, or physically robust; avoiding feelings of lethargy, weakness, or ill health

Cognitive Goals

Exploration — Satisfying one's curiosity about personally meaningful events; avoiding a sense of being uninformed or not knowing what's going on

Understanding — Gaining knowledge or making sense out of something; avoiding misconceptions, erroneous beliefs, or feelings of confusion

Intellectual Creativity — Engaging in activities involving original thinking or novel or interesting ideas; avoiding mindless or familiar ways of thinking

Positive Self-Evaluations — Maintaining a sense of self-confidence, pride, or self-worth; avoiding feelings of failure, guilt, or incompetence

Subjective Organization Goals

Unity — Experiencing a profound or spiritual sense of connectedness, harmony, or oneness with people, nature, or a greater power; avoiding feelings of psychological disunity or disorganization

Transcendence — Experiencing optimal or extraordinary state of functioning; avoiding feeling trapped within the boundaries of ordinary experience

Self-Assertive Social Relationship Goals

Individuality
Feeling unique, special, or different; avoiding similarity or conformity with others

Self-Determination
Experiencing a sense of freedom to act or make choices; avoiding the feeling of being pressured, constrained or coerced

Superiority
Comparing favorably to others in terms of winning, status, success; avoiding unfavorable comparisons with others

Resource Acquisition
Obtaining approval, support, assistance, advice, or validation from others; avoiding social disapproval or rejection

Integrative Social Relationship Goals

Belongingness
Building or maintaining attachments, friendships, intimacy, or a sense of community; avoiding feelings of social isolation or separateness

Social Responsibility
Keeping interpersonal commitments, meeting social role obligations, and conforming to social and moral rules; avoiding social transgressions and unethical or illegal conduct

Equity
Promoting fairness, justice, reciprocity, or equality; avoiding unfair or unjust actions

Resource Provision
Giving approval, support, assistance, advice, or validation to others; avoiding selfish or uncaring behavior

Task Goals

Mastery
Meeting a challenging standard of achievement or improvement; avoiding incompetence, mediocrity, or decrements in performance

Task Creativity
Engaging in activities involving artistic expression or creativity; avoiding tasks that do not provide opportunities for creative action

Management
Maintaining order, organization, or productivity in daily life tasks; avoiding sloppiness, inefficiency, or disorganization

Material Gain
Increasing the amount of money or tangible goods one has; avoiding the loss of money or material possessions

Safety
Being unharmed; physically secure, and free from risk; avoiding threatening, depriving, or harmful circumstances

Note. From "A Taxonomy of Human Goals and Some Possible Applications" by M. E. Ford and C. W. Nichols, 1987, in *Humans as Self-Constructing Living Systems: Putting the Framework to Work* (pp. 88–89), edited by M. E. Ford and D. H. Ford, Hillsdale, NJ: Erlbaum. Reprinted by permission.

goal attainment. It would thus appear that maintenance of goal-oriented behavior (effort, persistence, and direction) will occur to the degree that motivation for goal attainment can be instilled, elicited, and sustained.

Which particular goals or subgoals are pursued at any given time, and in what order, depends upon a host of individual and contextual influences, including a number of qualities of the goals themselves—their relevance, importance, attainability, and emotional salience of accomplishing them (Ford, 1992). Goal achievement is a consequence of these goal features; the motivational and commitment concerns considered previously; the individual's possession of relevant, goal-requisite resources; and the perception of self-efficacy (i.e., that he or she possesses such resources and skills).

Brunstein (1993), Emmons (1993), and Omodei and Wearing (1990) have all shown that progression toward significant goals is closely tied to a sense of long-term well-being. In aiding such goal-oriented progress, Emmons (1993) has recommended that change agents first seek to identify inappropriate client goals:

> Identification of goals that are overvalued, undervalued, unrealistic, conflict producing, or self-defeating would be the first step in designing an appropriate, workable intervention that would enable an individual to experience greater self-efficacy and positive states of well-being. The replacement of avoidant with approach goals or extreme high-level or low-level goals with mid-level goals may both be effective starting points for treatment. (p. 17)

Beyond giving adequate attention to modification of inappropriate goals, change agents may use a wide variety of overt and covert approaches to facilitate goal establishment, progression, and attainment. Even the act of contemplating goal progress and success may serve this purpose:

> When individuals think about possible outcomes in a concrete and systematic manner, they are much more likely to perform such actions in the future. Simply thinking about the processes needed to reach a particular goal enhances individuals' motivation to behave in certain ways and leads to effective self-regulatory strate-

gies. . . . Mental simulation makes the occurrence of events seem more likely, helps to establish and refine plans, evokes affective responses, and confirms that certain steps are essential to obtain a desired outcome. (Ward & Hudson, 1998, p. 704)

Clearly, attention to goal setting and attainment is central to any efforts to minimize client ambivalence, reluctance, and resistance. Following appropriate goal setting, motivation to change will not only be heightened, it will be sustained to the degree that the client believes he or she possesses the requisite goal attainment abilities (i.e., his or her sense of self-efficacy).

SELF-EFFICACY

Self-efficacy refers to one's beliefs in one's capabilities to organize and carry out courses of action necessary to produce given results. It is a self-perception not so much of one's skills per se but of one's ability to use whatever skills one possesses toward specific ends.

Self-efficacy may be distinguished from the domain of goals in that goals refer to one's aims, intentions, and hoped-for accomplishments. Self-efficacy is belief in one's ability to achieve given goals. Efficacy beliefs substantially influence thought processes, the intensity and persistence of motivation, and emotional state. All three of these sequelae in turn influence subsequent goal attainment. Perhaps most consequential is the effect of self-efficacy on motivation. Bandura (1997) has commented that

people who have strong beliefs in their capabilities approach difficult tasks as challenges to be mastered rather than as threats to be avoided. They set themselves challenging goals and maintain strong commitment to them. They invest a high level of effort in what they do and heighten their effort in the face of failures or setbacks. They remain task-focused and think strategically in the face of difficulties. They attribute failure to insufficient effort, which supports a success orientation. . . . They approach potential stressors or threats with the confidence that they can exercise control over them. . . . These findings offer substantial support for the view that beliefs of personal efficacy are active contributors to, rather than mere inert predictors of, human attainments. (p. 39)

Self-efficacy beliefs vary along a number of dimensions. Their *level* may entail simple challenges, moderately difficult demands, or complex challenges. Efficacy beliefs also vary in their *generality*. Individuals may perceive themselves as efficacious across a limited range of activities or across an array of areas of functioning. Finally, efficacy beliefs vary in *strength,* or the tenacity with which they are held. Some beliefs are weak and easily negated by disconfirming evidence. Others are held onto and accompanied by perseverant behavior in the face of severe difficulties and obstacles. The consequences of varying levels, generality, and strength of efficacy beliefs are broad and deep:

> People's beliefs in their efficacy have diverse effects. Such beliefs influence the courses of action people choose to pursue, how much effort they put forth in given endeavors, how long they will persevere in the face of obstacle and failures, their resilience to adversity, whether their thought patterns are self-hindering or self-aiding, how much stress and depression they experience in coping with taxing environmental demands, and the level of accomplishments they realize.
> (Bandura, 1997, p. 3)

These diverse claims regarding the positive consequences of efficacy beliefs are well supported by a large number of evaluation studies involving a broad and varied array of client disorders. These include anxiety and phobic reactions (Williams, 1995), depression (Maddux & Meier, 1995), smoking (Coelho, 1984), eating disorders (Schneider & Agras, 1985), alcohol and drug abuse (Sitharthan & Kavanagh, 1990), and a variety of physical health disorders (Schwartzer & Fuchs, 1995).

Motivated by these positive findings, researchers have devoted considerable attention to identifying and developing the means to facilitate high levels of strongly held and broadly applied self-efficacy beliefs. Three strategies, each implemented by a variety of tactics, have received particular attention. In ascending order of their apparent efficacy, they are verbal persuasion, vicarious experiences, and enactive mastery experiences.

Verbal persuasion primarily involves affirming, "you can do it" communications from significant others to the person involved. The credibility and skill level of the persuaders loom large, as does the nature of the relationship between the parties:

> People are inclined to trust evaluations of their capabilities by those who are themselves skilled in the activity, have access to some objective predictors of performance capability, or possess a rich fund of knowledge gained from observing and comparing many different aspirants and their later accomplishments. (Bandura, 1997, p. 105)

Efficacy appraisals from significant others are most likely to be believed, accepted, and considered a cause for action by the target person when such appraisals only moderately exceed what the individual has accomplished previously. Inflated appraisals, in contrast, are associated with greater potential for failure, along with decreases in self-efficacy beliefs and appraisal source credibility.

A rich literature on modeling, imitation, and observational learning suggests that the provision of relevant *vicarious experiences* is a second useful strategy for establishing and encouraging growth of self-efficacy beliefs. Seeing others similar to oneself accomplish a task helps engender the belief that one is able to do likewise. Such outcomes have been shown to be more likely the more similar the observer is to the model (e.g., sex, age, social status), the more confident the model, and the greater the model's success at goal attainment when several successful models are observed. Observational learning is also greater when the model or models are shown overcoming difficulties on their way to successful task performance (coping modeling) rather than engaging in task attainment free of difficulty (mastery modeling) and when the observer is more uncertain about his or her own task-relevant capabilities. An interesting and successful tactical use of the vicarious experience strategy is self-modeling (Dowrick, 1983, 1991). Here, persons who show capability deficiency or weakness are helped by a variety of external means to perform the given task more competently than permitted by their own abilities. This attempt is videotaped, and all mistakes, hesitancies, and external aids are edited out, yielding a record of the performance task at a competence level exceeding expectations.

As is the case for viewing other models, self-modeling has been shown to enhance beliefs in one's own capabilities and successful task performance (Dowrick & Jesdale, 1990; Kahn, Kehle, Jenson, & Clark, 1990).

Most potent in the effort to enhance self-efficacy is task success itself. Bandura (1997) terms these task successes *enactive mastery experiences:*

> Enactive mastery experiences are the most influential
> source of efficacy information because they provide the
> most authentic evidence of whether one can muster
> whatever it takes to succeed. Successes build a robust
> belief in one's personal efficacy. Failures undermine it,
> especially if failures occur before a sense of efficacy is
> firmly established. A resilient sense of efficacy requires
> experience in overcoming obstacles through persever-
> ant effort. (p. 80)

The degree to which performance leads to enhanced self-efficacy is, in this cognitive approach, a matter beyond behavior's yielding successful task completion. Appraisal of self-efficacy is an inferential process involving the individual's weighing of the relative contributions of strengths and weaknesses to performance. Also helping determine efficacy beliefs are the perceived difficulty of the task, the amount of effort expended, the amount of aid received, and other qualities of the task-attainment attempt.

Many approaches to providing enactive mastery experiences exist. In sociocognitive theory as applied to the treatment of phobic disorders, for example, "guided mastery" or "participant modeling" is conducted as follows:

> In these procedures, the therapist first models the
> feared activities for the client. The appropriate coping
> behavior is then broken down into graded, attainable
> subtasks, which the therapist and client then perform
> together. If the client experiences difficulty with any of
> the specific subtasks, the therapist helps the client per-
> form the task by using a variety of aids and techniques,
> such as "graduated time" procedures in which the client
> performs the subtask for a shorter and more tolerable
> period. . . . When the client feels sufficiently effica-

cious, however, the therapist gradually withdraws the aids, and the client performs them independently.
Finally, the therapist and client collaborate on designing additional self-directed mastery experiences to further enhance the strength and generality of the client's self-efficacy for engaging in the feared activities. (Cervone & Scott, 1995, p. 367)

In addition to guided mastery and participant modeling, a host of other procedures embedded in a wide variety of psychotherapy, counseling, and educational approaches have targeted self-efficacy, though labeled otherwise. Beck, Rush, Shaw, and Emery's (1979) guided imagery technique, in which clients imagine approaching difficult tasks with thoughts of high efficacy, is one example. Maddi, Kahn, and Maddi's (1998) hardiness training is another. Here, "action plans" are developed and carried out to provide clients with a greater sense of perceived control and experience of task accomplishment. Homework or behavioral assignment techniques certainly fit here, especially when such assignments are graduated in difficulty and when their scheduling is yoked to subtask accomplishment. Kelly's (1955) use of fixed-role sketches is a good illustration. As Kelly noted in describing the consequences of successful role enactment, "Once a person can say, 'Look, I have changed, haven't I?' he is more able to say, 'I can change' " (p. 372). The behavioral rehearsal or role-play component of so many behavioral and psychoeducational interventions is a further example. All of these techniques provide individuals with enactive mastery experiences and, as a consequence, heightened levels of perceived self-efficacy.

CONCLUSIONS

I have focused in this chapter on motivational enhancement strategies and tactics as they might optimally be utilized during phases before and early on in therapy. Given the dramatically high "no show" and "early attrition" dropout rates noted in chapter 1, it is clear that motivation-increasing and resistance-reducing efforts at these stages are crucial to the attainment of therapeutic goals. Attention to an array of precursor variables, use of motivational interviewing philosophy and techniques, extended focus on client goal setting and goal attainment, and energetic use of means to support and encourage client self-efficacy are the major motivation-enhancing approaches.

CHAPTER 3

Relationship Enhancement

As previously noted, in recent decades client resistance has come to be viewed more as an interpersonal than as an intrapsychic phenomenon. Resistance grows, many have held, primarily from errors, strains, ruptures, and other similar negative events and forces in the interaction of therapist and client, rather than being a singular quality of the latter's psyche (Gelso & Hayes, 1998; Langs, 1981; Rappaport, 1997). It is not much of a leap to place the therapist-client relationship at the center of such an interactional view of resistance. Stated simply, a positive therapeutic relationship ought to minimize and mitigate client resistance and, almost by definition, negative relationship qualities ought likely not only reflect but also generate and intensify client resistance. Safran and Segal (1996) capture this perspective on resistance as relationship difficulty in their examination of "alliance ruptures":

> An alliance rupture can be defined as a point in the interaction between therapist and patient when the quality of the therapeutic alliance is strained or impaired. [Alliance ruptures] range from simple misunderstandings, quickly and easily resolved within a few moments, to more chronic problems in the therapeutic alliance which may extend over the course of one or more sessions, or over the course of the entire therapy. (p. 88)

In this interactional view of resistance—a virtual therapist and client duet—both parties contribute to relationship difficulties and hence resistance. When they do so, it is often in a reciprocal manner. Thus, ill-timed therapist interpretations or empathic failures may initiate client withdrawal of cooperation, reduced self-disclosure, or spotty attendance at sessions. These client behaviors in turn may generate further therapist-initiated contributions to client resistive behavior—in a kind of "negative feed-forward" loop. In contrast, when the quality of the relationship is decidedly positive, resistance is minimal or absent, and positive relationship quality is fostered. Safran and Segal describe this productive state of affairs:

> When there is a good therapeutic alliance there is an empathic resonance between therapist and patient. The therapist walks in the patient's shoes, feels affected emotionally by what the patient says, and finds that the patient responds to the therapist's empathic comments in ways that acknowledge the feelings of being understood. The therapist and patient thus respond to each other as if they were dancing. The patient says something and then waits for the therapist's response, the therapist speaks and then is open to the patient's response. The patient's comments appear to flow directly in response to the therapist's comments and questions. There is thus a sense of building or creating something together. (1996, pp. 89–90)

From Freud's (1910/1953) early comments on analyst-patient collaboration and Carl Rogers' (1957) writings on core facilitative conditions to more recent observations regarding the power of the "liking bond" (Gelso & Hayes, 1998) and the technology of relationship enhancement (Goldstein & Higgenbotham, 1991), wide agreement exists that resistance is minimized and progress maximized when patient and therapist are relating well.

RELATIONSHIP AND OUTCOME

The therapist-client relationship, as it relates to the eventual outcome of the therapy, has been viewed in three different, if complementary, ways. One is of relationship as the *source* of client change. In the early Rogerian (Rogers, 1957) view of psychotherapy, for example, the core facilitative conditions of the therapist's contribution to the relationship were all that were "necessary and sufficient" for positive outcomes to ensue. In a second view, a positive therapist-client relationship is seen as necessary but insufficient. The therapist's techniques have their impact in the context of the relationship. As is characteristic of early writings in behavior modification and cognitive-behavioral approaches, the therapist-client relationship is seen as prerequisite and instrumental—as leverage and as an *enabler* of the therapeutic process. In the third perspective on relationship and outcome, the relationship is conceptualized as a *behavior sample*. How the client "comes on to" or relates to the therapist is treated as a microcosm or isomorphic reflection of the client's other, real-world relationships. The core psychoanalytic concept of transference exemplifies such a perspective.

Whether seen as source, enabler, or sample, a favorable relationship reduces resistance and facilitates a positive therapeutic outcome. Taylor (1984) does not overstate in claiming that

> the relationship between the therapist and the client is
> the foundation of the therapeutic enterprise. The nature
> of this relationship is the therapist's most important
> means of effecting client change, and it determines the
> success or failure of the therapy. (p. 219)

The therapist-client relationship is parsimoniously defined following Gelso and Hayes (1998) as "the feelings and attitudes that therapist and client have toward one another, and the manner in which these are stressed" (p. 6). Much has been written in recent years regarding relationship (e.g., the working alliance, the transference, and the real relationship; Gaston, 1990; Lambert & Bergin, 1994; Rappaport, 1997). Further, at least in their rationales, different therapies emphasize different components. For example, the humanistic approach stresses the real (authentic) therapist-client relationship; the psychoanalytic, the transference relationship; the cognitive-behavioral, the working alliance. In each instance, it has been shown either empirically or clinically—across components, types of therapy, types of patients, and types of outcome measures—that the relationship is a major determinant of outcome.

The positive association between quality of the therapist-client relationship and therapeutic outcome—sometimes demonstrated correlationally, other times, causally—has been reported in conjunction with short-term dynamic psychotherapy (Koss & Shiang, 1994); interpersonal psychotherapy (Rounsaville, Dolinsky, Babor, & Meyer, 1987); time-limited manualized drug therapy (Luborsky, 1994); psychoanalytically oriented therapy (Foreman & Marmar, 1985); person-centered humanistic therapy (Tageson, 1982); group therapy (Yalom & Lieberman, 1971); behavior therapy (Sloane, 1975); cognitive-behavioral therapy (Murphy, Cramer, & Lillie, 1984); and cognitive therapy (Gaston, Marmar, & Ring, 1989), as well as with other approaches. Further, as noted, the association holds across types of patients: depressed (Marmar, Gaston, Gallagher, & Thompson, 1989); obsessive-compulsive (Rabavilas, Boulougouris, & Perissaki, 1979); agoraphobic (Williams & Chambless, 1990); delinquent (Alexander, 1997); schizophrenic (Frank & Gunderson, 1990); and others. It is a robust finding indeed, evidenced in both traditional literature reviews of the relationship-outcome connection (e.g., Luborsky, 1994; Orlinsky, Grawe, & Parks, 1994) and in formal meta-analyses (e.g., Horvath & Symonds, 1991). Because the present text is on resistance, it is important to note that the consistent findings regarding the therapist-client relationship also often include evidence that a poor quality relationship leads, via negative therapeutic events (strain, misunderstanding, dislike, ruptures), to a correspondingly poor therapeutic outcome (Foreman & Marmar, 1985; Henry, Schacht, & Strupp, 1986; Kiesler & Watkins, 1989; Tasca & McMullen, 1992).

Relationship ruptures, suggest Safran and Muran (2000), are of two subtypes, withdrawal and confrontation. In withdrawal, the client disengages from the therapist, perhaps subtly, at times dramatically. In confrontation, the resistance is a more overt expression of reluctance, resentment, or even anger. Bordin's (1994) description of the therapist-client relationship as a "working alliance" sees the alliance as resting on a shared view of therapeutic goals, and the tasks necessary to reach those goals, as well as on the strength of the bond between therapist and client. Goals, tasks, and bonds may each be the locus of relationship ruptures. The degree to which such resistances in fact appear, and the opportunity their appearance provides as a means of dealing with core client concerns, varies with the degree of client disturbance. As Bordin observes:

> To me, the most important element in dealing with strain and ruptures in the working alliance is that they represent prime opportunities for change with persons whose psychological state creates the conditions most recalcitrant to alteration. With many garden varieties of clients, a basically adequate alliance will foster change with little accompanying strain or rupture. These are

the mildly neurotic. . . . As we move past these groups in terms of severity, we enter the region where change will depend heavily on the utilization of strain and rupture episodes to foster the work of an individual overcoming firmly established inner obstacles toward change. Finally, there is a group so severely deprived in their object relations capacities—psychotic, schizophrenic, borderline—for whom the development of the capacity to enter into an elementary working alliance is a critical, extended, and painful process. (1994, p. 27)

Bordin is correct: Rupture repair and concomitant relationship building can be both crucial to outcome and difficult to achieve. However, what may fairly be called a technology of relationship enhancement does exist and is the main topic of the rest of this chapter. It is a technology with demonstrated and anticipated potential for improving the quality of the therapist-client relationship, reducing the resistances often inherent in such interactions, and thus contributing to a positive therapeutic outcome.

RELATIONSHIP-ENHANCEMENT TECHNOLOGY

Influences on the quality of the therapist-client relationship begin to operate well before the two parties meet, during the contemplation, referral, intake, and assessment stages of the client's treatment career. It is during these pretreatment periods that relationship-enhancement efforts will optimally begin.

Client Structuring

Operationally, structuring a client so that he or she will like or be attracted to the therapist is, quite simply, a matter of (a) telling the client that he or she will like the therapist (direct structuring), (b) briefly describing certain positive characteristics of the therapist (trait structuring), or (c) clarifying what the client can realistically anticipate will go on in meetings with the therapist (role-expectancy structuring). Each of these structuring procedures seeks to move the client's expectations and feelings about his or her relationship with the therapist in a positive direction, it is hoped thus reducing resistance to change and increasing client openness to the therapist's influence. Studies have shown that what partners believe about each other may be more important than objective reality in influencing relationship satisfaction (Hendrick, Hendrick, & Adler, 1988).

In one of the first uses of direct structuring to strengthen client attraction to the therapist, new clients at a counseling center were first given certain tests that asked for information about the kind of therapist they would prefer—his or her behavior, expectations, goals, and so on. Shortly after this testing, clients were told the following:

> We have carefully examined the tests you took in order to assign you to a therapist whom you would like to work with most. We usually can't match a patient and therapist the way they want most, but for you we have almost exactly the kind of therapist you described. (The tester then showed the client how well his test results describing his preferred therapist apparently matched other information purportedly indicating the actual behavior, expectations and goals of the therapist with whom he would be meeting.) As a matter of fact, the matching of the kind of person you wanted to work with and the kind of person Mr. _____ is, is so close that it hardly ever happens. What's even more, he has often described the kind of patient he likes to work with most as someone just like you in many respects. You two should get along extremely well. (Goldstein, 1971, p. 21)

No actual matching of client preferences with therapist characteristics was performed. Clients participated in the structuring procedure, then each was assigned to a therapist whose turn it was for a new client. Nevertheless, such structuring led clients to show increased liking of their therapists and increased openness about their problems. Thus, clients' belief that therapists would be the kinds of people they would like was enough to influence their actual attraction toward them and to facilitate the therapeutic process.

The enhancing effect on both attraction and openness has been shown to be even stronger when trait structuring of the client is conducted. In trait structuring, persons such as the referral source or agency intake worker describe qualities of the therapist to the client before client and therapist actually meet. Once again, the effect of these procedures on the attraction that develops is quite strong, even though the therapist characteristics described might in fact not be present. Which particular therapist characteristics are selected to be described to the client is an important matter. In most uses of trait structuring, the two therapist traits chosen have been warmth and experience. The first of these tells the client something important about how comfortable she or he is likely to feel during the helping process. The second gives the client information about the likely positive outcome of this process. Both items, therefore, enhance client attraction to the therapist. The statement that follows is an example of trait structuring of therapist warmth and experience:

> The therapist has been engaged in the practice of therapy for over 20 years and has lectured and taught at some of the country's leading universities and medical schools. Questionnaires submitted to the therapist's colleagues seem to reveal that he is a rather warm person, industrious, critical, practical and determined.
> (Goldstein, 1971, p. 50)

Trait structuring has also been used successfully "in reverse" to increase therapist attraction toward the client (Goldstein, 1971). Here qualities of the client are emphasized that lead the therapist to anticipate that the client will be "a good patient." The type of problem the client supposedly has, the diagnosis, and his or her motivation to work to improve are examples of positively structured client traits that have been communicated to the therapist. Indeed, as discussed later in this chapter, it is probably even more important for the therapist to perceive the help seeker as an attractive client than it is for the client to see the therapist in a favorable light, given the relatively greater power of the therapist's expectations to influence treatment outcome.

A great deal of psychological research has been conducted to assess the effects of leading a person to believe she or he is similar to a stranger in important attitudes, background, or values on her or his liking for that stranger when they meet. This research convincingly shows that the greater the structured similarity, the greater the attraction to the other person. When other people's beliefs or attitudes agree with one's own, it may satisfy one's need to be logical and interpret the environment correctly.

Or similarity may produce attraction because we assume that people who agree with us will also like us, and we tend to like those who like us (Condon & Crano, 1988). The positive effect of structured similarity on attraction has also been found to operate in the therapist-client relationship. Largely for this reason, great use has been made in recent years of certain types of paraprofessional helpers—that is, persons who are lacking in formal training or degrees but who possess beliefs, personal backgrounds, and lifestyles similar to those of the persons they are seeking to help. The similarities between paraprofessional therapists and the people they serve, like structured similarity, enhance the quality of the therapeutic relationship.

Whether the therapist is formally credentialed or paraprofessional, several findings seem to support the link between similarity and improved relationship. Murphy and Strong (1972) examined the impact of therapist self-disclosures of similarity on perceived attractiveness in simulated helping interviews. Procedurally, they varied the number of self-disclosing statements revealing information about the therapist similar to that for the client. Findings showed that an intermediate number of such disclosures (four, rather than zero or eight) most effectively facilitated positive client ratings of therapist empathy, regard, and congruence, as well as client self-disclosure. Using similar designs, Hoffman-Graff (1975) found significant perceived similarity effects on client attraction to the therapist and client return rate for a second interview. Perceived similarity, apparently, influences both liking the therapist (e.g., attraction, regard) and willingness to be influenced (e.g., self-disclosure, return for sessions).

Thus far, the discussion has shown that direct structuring and trait structuring for warmth, experience, and similarity can have attraction-increasing effects. So, too, can a final type of structuring: role-expectancy structuring. Failure to appear for the first scheduled psychotherapy session, early attrition for those who do start, and substandard participation during sessions have each been shown to result from discrepant expectations held by therapist and client. As Higginbotham, West, and Forsyth (1988) observe:

> Mutuality or congruence of client and counselor role
> expectations significantly influences the content, dura-

tion, and outcome of counseling. Conversely, failure to confirm the client's expectations of the therapist's personal qualities, tactics, pronouncements, and prescriptions results in negative consequences to the therapeutic relationship and potential behavior change. (p. 127)

Whereas direct and trait structuring mostly concern telling the client something about the kind of person the therapist is, role-expectancy structuring focuses on what the therapist (and what the client) actually do when they meet. If, because of misinformation or lack of information about what to expect, the client later experiences surprising or confusing events during meetings with the therapist, negative feelings will result. Events that confirm the client's expectancies increase his or her attraction to the therapist. For example, many new patients come to psychotherapy with expectations based on what they judge to be similar relationships, such as the relationship they have with their medical doctors. During doctor visits, the patient typically presents a physical problem briefly, is asked a series of questions by the physician, and is then authoritatively told what to do. When the client with "medical expectations" starts psychotherapy, he or she is in for some surprises. The client describes a psychological problem and sits back, awaiting the therapist's questions and eventual advice. If the therapeutic approach involved is one or another form of psychodynamic, insight-oriented treatment, the therapist, unlike the general physician, wants the client to explore feelings, examine history, and speculate about the causes of the problem. When such important role expectations differ, the relationship suffers. This is but one of several ways in which client and therapist can differ in their anticipations of how each will behave.

Prior structuring of expectations has been shown to contribute to increased attraction and a more lasting and fruitful therapist-client relationship. Such role-expectancy structuring has been accomplished by providing the client with a structuring interview (also called an anticipatory socialization interview or a role induction interview) before the first meeting with the therapist. In this interview, an intake worker or another therapist provides specific information about what the prospective client can expect to occur in psychotherapy. Topics covered include how much talking the client is expected to do, how the problem will be assessed,

whether or not to expect direct advice, the amount of responsibility assigned the client in the "work" of therapy, potential emotional discomfort, and so forth. Following is an excerpt from an
interview in which a therapist explains to a prospective client what
he or she can expect to occur in psychotherapy:

> Now, what is therapy about?* What is going on? Well,
> for one thing, I have been talking a great deal; in treat-
> ment your doctor won't talk very much. The reason I
> am talking now is that I want to explain these things to
> you. There is equally good reason that the doctor in
> treatment does not say much. Everyone expects to tell
> the psychiatrist about his problem and then have him
> give advice which will solve everything just like that.
> This isn't true; it just doesn't work like that. . . . Before
> you came here you got advice from all kinds of people.
> . . . If all of the advice you have received had helped,
> odds are that you wouldn't be here. Your doctor wants
> to help you to figure out what you really want to do—
> what the best solution is for you. It's his job not to give
> advice but to help you find out for yourself how you
> are going to solve your problem.

> Now, what goes on in treatment itself? What is it that
> you talk about? What is it that you do? How does it
> work? Well, for one thing, you will talk about your
> wishes, both now and in the past. . . .You will find
> that with your doctor you will be able to talk about
> what is right or what is wrong for you or what the best
> solution would be. Talking is very important because
> he wants to help you get at what you really want. . . .
> The doctor's job is to help you make the decision. . . .
> Most of us are not honest with ourselves. We try to kid
> ourselves, and it's your doctor's job to make you aware
> of when you are kidding yourself. He is not going to
> try to tell you what he thinks but he will point out to
> you how two things you are saying just don't fit
> together.

---

*From "Anticipatory Socialization for Psychotherapy" by M. T. Orne & P. H.
Wender, 1968, *American Journal of Psychiatry, 124,* pp. 1205–1206. Copyright
1968 by the American Psychiatric Association. Reprinted by permission.

The patient . . . sometimes feels worse and discouraged at some stages of treatment. You know, you'll feel you're not getting anywhere, your doctor is a fool, and there's no point in this, and so on. These very feelings are often good indications that you are working and that it's uncomfortable. It is very important that you don't give in to these temporary feelings when they come up.

Say whatever comes to your mind, even if you think it is trivial or unimportant. It doesn't matter. It is still important to say it. And if you think it is going to bother your doctor, that doesn't matter either; you still say it.

So, just like the [keeping of] appointments, we make an absolute rule not to think ahead about what you'll say and therefore protect yourself from facing important things. Say whatever is on the top of your mind, no matter what. (Orne & Wender, 1968, pp. 1205–1206)

Employing such pretherapy role-expectancy structuring, Hoehn-Saric et al. (1964) showed that recipients, in contrast to nonstructured control-group clients, had enhanced scores on relationship, participation, and outcome criteria. Perhaps of special relevance to resistance, subjects provided with role-expectancy structuring were also significantly more likely to continue in treatment. Similarly, Jacobs, Charles, Jacobs, Weinstein, and Mann (1972) found a positive role-expectancy structuring effect on attendance for treatment. While such structuring is not always successful with regard to participation, relationship, or outcome (Yalom, Houts, Newell, & Rand, 1967), a number of other investigations have confirmed and elaborated the original Hoehn-Saric et al. findings (i.e., Berrigan & Garfield, 1981; Strupp & Bloxom, 1973; Weighill, Hodge, & Peck, 1983).

Whether or not pretherapy role induction is provided to the client, it remains incumbent on the therapist, at the very outset of treatment, to educate the client regarding what to expect. Neuman (1994) sketches this need clearly:

Clients often do not understand what to expect when they enter therapy, partly as a function of the diversity of the field, partly due to misconceptions borne of sensationalized or unflattering portrayals of therapists on television and in movies, and somewhat as a function of their own biases and misconceptions (e.g., "Therapy is like a magic pill. I just show up and the therapist will say all the right things to make me better.") . . . This would include an explanation of the model of treatment . . . a preview about the expected length and substance of the course of therapy, and a discussion about the roles and responsibilities of both the therapist and the client. (p. 57)

In summary, structuring can lead to an enhanced relationship in the form of increased attraction of the client toward the therapist, whether such structuring is a straightforward statement that the client will probably like the helper (direct structuring), a description of certain of the helper's positive qualities or of helper-client similarity (trait structuring), or an explanation of the events and behaviors one should expect in the relationship (role-expectancy structuring).

Therapist-Client Negotiation of Meaning

Another method to enhance helping relationships involves purposeful negotiation of the inevitable differences that exist between therapist and client.* Differences in social status, gender, age, values, ethnicity, and so forth may subvert the development of the therapeutic alliance unless resolved in the initial meetings. Such differences are not trivial; they influence fundamental helping processes such as the language forms people use to communicate and the meaning attached to the presenting problem. This section concerns ways to create and sustain cooperative conversation, particularly when therapist and client are of unequal status or are culturally dissimilar. Three points are made: First, therapists must access culture-specific knowledge if they are to interpret accurately and respond to the social meaning of spoken information. Second, they must explore the meaning of client nonverbal communications, given what they reveal about client feelings toward the helping relationship. Third, they must

---

*A more exhaustive version of this section was prepared by Nick Higgenbotham for "Relationship-Enhancement Methods" by A. P. Goldstein and H. N. Higgenbotham, in F. H. Kanfer and A. P. Goldstein (Eds.), *Helping People Change* (pp. 29–32), 1991, New York: Allyn and Bacon. Copyright © 1991 by Allyn and Bacon. Adapted by permission.

negotiate the meaning of the illness event or problem in order to set a mutually agreeable course of treatment.

When client and therapist face each other at their first session, each brings linguistic abilities tuned to the conventions of his or her own speech community. Mutually understood conversation becomes possible only when the speakers are able to negotiate a common interpretation of the signals used in their verbal and nonverbal exchanges. Gumprez (1982) found that people socialized in different speech communities will signal their intended meaning by following different unspoken ground rules. Cues to signal the meaning of speech include eye contact, gestures, postural shifts, changes in voice tone and loudness, how questions are posed, and other subtleties. In our highly mobile and urbanized society, communication with speakers of differing sociocultural backgrounds is the rule rather than the exception. Clinicians must identify breakdowns in conversational coordination and deftly negotiate with the client accurate interpretations of speech signals in order to establish and maintain fluent conversation.

Higginbotham et al. (1988) describe how therapists may overcome language barriers with clients and gain conversational cooperation. First, the clinician carefully monitors initial verbal exchanges with the client, listening for an uneven flow of talk; hesitance; or abrupt changes in sentence rhythm, pitch, and intonation. These uncomfortable moments alert the clinician to the breakdown in rhythmic exchange of signals between self and speech partner. When partners miss each other's cues regarding how what is said is to be understood, it is clear that they have not yet agreed on what activity is unfolding and the ground rules by which it is to be carried out.

When the clinician detects uncomfortable moments, he or she refrains from placing blame for the poor communication because it is understood that troublesome interactions are jointly produced by the speech partners. Instead of viewing the client as uncooperative, hostile, or of low intelligence, the clinician explores other reasons. There may be cultural differences in speech conventions. The client may feel that the relationship is accelerating too quickly and with too much self-disclosure. Discomfort is expressed through hesitant speech and anxious gestures as the client acts to avoid intimacy. Or, despite good intentions, the clinician and client may not have negotiated a common framework for agreeing on the nature and direction of their conversation. Thus, with each client the clinician must prepare to undertake a momentary diagnosis of the conversation— in the midst of the uncomfortable moment as it happens.

How can therapist and client better decipher each other's messages? One strategy is "small talk," active searching for personal similarities, mutual interests, or shared experiences. Self-disclosure appropriate to the partners' expectations helps identify commonalities. However, active listening and self-disclosure, which enhance feelings of community and help coordinate interactions, are generalized insights rather than discrete skills. Erickson and Shultz (1982) point out that clinical training that approaches cross-cultural communication as simply skills training—that is, how to talk with people of African, Asian, Chicano, or other minority descent—will only reinforce racial, ethnic, and social class stereotypes (see also Pederson, 1986). Moreover, if therapists attempt too quickly to elicit personal dialogue from clients by offering self-revealing statements or asking intimate questions, then clients are apt to feel threatened and compensate by decreasing affiliation with the therapist (Capella, 1981; Derlega & Chaikin, 1975). Therapist openness, steady gaze, forward body lean, and other nonverbal gestures to increase contact may actually prompt reactions of extreme avoidance among some clients. Such therapist approaches have been found to increase delusional activity and negative self-disclosure, postural rigidity, and nonfunctional nervous movements among psychiatric inpatients (e.g., Fairbanks, McGuire, & Harris, 1982).

Clinicians strain not only to interpret spoken messages but also to read the client's face and body for nonverbal cues that reveal the affect, intensity, and sincerity of the accompanying words. The helping relationship is enhanced when the therapist assumes the role of "discrepancy detector" and becomes sensitive to inconsistencies between nonverbal and verbal communication channels, as well as among the nonverbal channels themselves (face, body, and voice quality). The face is not the place to look for the speaker's true feelings because people learn to monitor and control emotional expression in that channel. People are less aware of the information they convey through body channels—hands, feet, and legs. Consequently, the affect sent is less disguised or controlled (DePaulo, Zuckerman, & Rosenthal, 1980; Ekman & Friesen, 1969). Experimental studies of deception have shown that subjects induced to lie will blink at a higher rate, hesitate longer before answering, groom and touch themselves more frequently, and have more frequent errors and hesitations in speech (Kraut, 1980).

Just as uncomfortable moments of conversation alert the therapist that mutual understanding is deteriorating, so too do discrepant nonverbal cues and cues of deception signal moments when clients' unspoken emotions more accurately describe their experience of the therapeutic relationship than does the content of their speech. When these inconsistencies remain hidden, unsatisfying patterns of communication result. The therapeutic task is, therefore, to pinpoint these moments and then to negotiate with the client his or her definition of the situational and affective meaning associated with those unspoken reactions. A therapist sensitive to nonverbal communication will penetrate the client's masked and unspoken emotions, and will strive to coordinate his or her rhythm of therapeutic communication with the system of cues sent by the client (see Higginbotham et al., 1988, pp. 93–103).

Another area of negotiation in the therapist-client relationship concerns how the presenting problem will be interpreted and managed. Cognitive therapists in the tradition of George Kelly and Jerome Frank endorse as a universal condition of healing the sufferer's and therapist's willingness to share a conceptual framework. Healing transpires when the therapist helps the sufferer draw on this conceptual framework, to translate the cognitive expressions of demoralization into verbal referents and assumptions that are more meaningful and therefore more manageable. Meichenbaum (1977) states that therapist and client together fabricate a new explanation for the etiology and maintenance of maladaptive behavior and that the client implicitly accepts this new conceptualization as a byproduct of therapeutic interaction.

The construction of a new problem interpretation can and should be made an explicit aim of the negotiation cycle. It is recommended that therapist and client undertake four clinical steps to arrive at a mutual understanding of the problem and a treatment plan. First, the therapist draws out the client's implicit theory or explanation of the problem. Probes are made of the client's specific propositions about the dysfunction: (a) why it is happening; (b) why the symptoms have assumed a particular form; (c) how the dysfunction works psychologically or physically to produce its effects; (d) how long it will last; and (e) the most suitable treatment and expected benefits (see Kleinman, 1980, pp. 105–106).

The second step involves therapist disclosure of selected portions of the clinical theory with which he or she will interpret the client's presenting problem. The theory should be conveyed in nontechnical and direct terms for each of the five aforementioned propositions about the problem (Kleinman, Eisenberg, & Good, 1978).

Third, client and therapist examine the discrepancies and "fit" between their respective problem explanations. This examination brings into focus any conflicts in problem conception that will require clarification and further explanation or frank negotiation to resolve. However, the therapist should keep in mind that the client may use the same terms but define them differently, may have the same problem definition but infer that it has different causes, or may steadfastly avoid using a term because of stigma attached by his or her social group (Harwood, 1981).

The fourth step requires therapist and client to bridge the differences in their understanding and expectations or to break off the relationship. A further circular exchange of information, clarifying terms and concepts, may prove differences to be more apparent than real. "Conceptual translation" may be required, where the speaker explains the meaning of his or her concepts through the use of metaphors, images, or idioms the other is known to understand. For example, Nichter described lithium's effects to a manic patient by using the patient's own image of her nervous system as a network of electrical wires (Nichter & Trockman, 1983). Ultimately, the client may adopt the helper's explanation in addition to (or instead of) his or her original model, retain the original model, or devise a totally new explanation (Kleinman, 1980). Successful negotiation is likely to produce a satisfying working relationship and agreement about the most effective treatment method and what constitutes a beneficial outcome. Failure to agree on a common problem conception is best handled through referral to another care provider who may be able to match the client's orientation more closely.

Imitation

In addition to client structuring and therapist-client negotiation of meaning, a third approach to relationship enhancement originates with research on imitation. Essentially, increasing attraction to the therapist through imitation involves exposing the client to a person (a model) who plays the part of a client who likes the therapist and clearly says so. This approach is also called modeling or observational learning. In the typical use of imitation, an audiotape or videotape of the model client is played for the real client. The content of such tapes is usually part of an actual or constructed counseling or psychotherapy session between the model and the therapist. The client simply listens to or observes the tape(s) and then later meets with the therapist. The following is an excerpt from such an attraction-imitation tape, a tape that in its entirety includes a dozen high-attraction statements:

> How would I like my parents to be different? Well, I think mostly in the fact that they could've cared more, that they could have showed it, you know, been warmer and not so cold. That's mainly it. . . . You know, I guess I said this before, but *even though all you've been doing the past 5 or 10 minutes is asking me questions, I still for some reason or another feel comfortable talking to you and being honest about myself. I feel that you're warm and that you care.* (Goldstein, 1973, p. 216)

As suggested in the discussion of structuring, a change-enhancing relationship involves client attraction toward the therapist and therapist attraction toward the client. The more reciprocal or mutual the positive feelings, the more likely rapid progress toward client change. For this reason, imitation has also been used to increase therapist attraction to the client. The following transcript, adapted from Goldstein (1973), is part of a modeling tape designed for this purpose, a tape used successfully with therapists of several orientations. Each statement in italics depicts a model therapist expressing attraction, liking, or positive evaluation toward a client—that is, expressing the behaviors the listening therapists were to learn and imitate.

Therapist: Since this is our first interview, I'll be asking you about a number of different areas of your life. Why don't we start off by your telling me about your family?

Patient: My family. Well, you know sometimes . . . sometimes I think my family could do . . . just as well without me. You know. Like I'm a . . . useless sort of object that sort of sits around the house. When I . . . come home from work it's like . . . like there's nothing there.

Therapist: You don't feel that your family looks forward to your coming home at night?

Patient: Sometimes it . . . sometimes it seems that they don't even know when I'm home. Kids'll be running around and . . . my wife . . . well, sometimes the way she acts it would be better if I just stayed out. Some of the things that she gets into . . . Mmmmmmmmmmmmmm.

Therapist: *I'm not clear why your wife would act that way. I find you a rather easy person to talk with.* What kind of things does your wife get into?

Patient: I don't know. She's always yelling and screaming . . . wants me to do things when I come inside . . . always telling me I have this to do and that to do. She doesn't realize I just wanna come home and I wanna relax a little bit. Nah . . . I don't know how she can push me all the time . . . do this . . . do that . . . all the time.

Therapist: Sounds like marriage has been a lot of trouble for you.

Patient: Yeah. Yeah . . . really it . . . it was different before. When we first got married it was . . . it was nice. We went out and saw different people, did . . . did some things together. Got along pretty good, too. Didn't have all this that's going on now.

Therapist: *From our meeting so far, I'm finding it rather easy to get along with you, too.* I guess things aren't going very well with your wife now.

Patient: No . . . my wife changed. She got . . . she got different. Things started . . . you know . . . she started not to care about things. We couldn't go out as much. Then . . . then the babies came and then . . . wow . . . feeding them and taking care of them and doing all those things. Never had any time to do the things that we used to do together. You know, it's usually hard for me to talk about things like this, but it's easy talking to you. Like . . . you know when I'd come home from work . . . my wife . . . she'd be running around the house after the kids . . . and when I'd come in the door I'd get ignored, you know. No one says hello . . . no one asks you how you are.

Therapist: Somehow all this seemed to happen around the time the children came?

Patient: It . . . seems that way. Before we had the kids we didn't have these problems. Now it . . . it's just not the same.

Therapist: What about your parents, did your father . . . drink?

Patient: Oh, yeah. He . . . could down them with the best of them. My old lady will tell you that. Yeah, he really knew how to drink. Used to get into some terrible fights with my old lady, though. Boy . . . he'd come home . . . have a little too much in him . . . she'd really let him have it. I'd have to . . . pull the pillow up over my head so I wouldn't hear the noise. Couldn't get to sleep.

Therapist: Your mother was very hard on your father, then.

Patient: Yeah. She really used to get mad at him. You know, for drinking and all that. She used to yell at him. Get on his back all the time. Really be nasty to him. Maybe that's one of the reasons why he's 6 feet under right now.

Therapist: Sort of like the same thing your wife is doing to you?

Patient: Yeah. You're right. You really hit the nail on the head. You really understand what's going on. There's a lot of things about the two that are kind of the same. I think she's trying to do the same thing to me that my mother did to my father. Yell and fight . . . the yelling and carrying on. They'll both do it. Scream at you . . . and call you a drunk. Telling me I can't take on any responsibility. Always yelling about something. Money. Why don't you have more of it? Why can't we buy this? Why can't we buy that? I'm working . . . as hard as I can . . . and she does . . . she doesn't realize that. She thinks all I have to do is work . . . all the time. She thinks it's . . . it's easy for me to . . . to work every day. Always pushing me. I don't like to be pushed. I get . . . I'll get things done. But I have to work . . . at my own pace, otherwise . . . it just doesn't matter if I work or not, if I can't work at my own pace.

Therapist: *You seem to be really trying to make your marriage work. I respect people who really try like that.* It sounds like your wife and you just don't do things the same way.

Patient: Yeah. She's in her own world. She doesn't care about anything that I do . . . or say. She doesn't care about me or anyone else. Sometimes I just feel like getting up and leaving. There's nothing there any more.

Therapist: You'd like to just go away?

Patient: Mm-hmm.

Therapist: Have you ever done this?

Patient: Not for any long time. Used to . . . get away for a couple of days by myself. But I always ended up coming back because I had no one else to go to.

Therapist: *Well, now when you feel like that you can come see me.* You don't like being alone.

As the dialogue shows, imitation enhances attraction, but matters are not quite this simple. Each of us observes many people every day, but most of what we observe we do not imitate. We see expensively produced and expertly acted modeling displays of people buying things on television commercials, but more often than not we do not imitate them. People imitate others only under certain circumstances. We tend to imitate others with whom we can identify; thus, to encourage imitation, the client model should be the same sex and approximate age as the client whose attraction is to be increased. We are especially prone to imitate behavior we see leading to rewards that we, too, desire. Therefore, the most successful attraction-enhancing modeling is that in which the client model is rewarded by having his or her problems resolved. Further, it is not accidental that television commercials frequently involve repetition (particularly of the product's name); imitation often increases with repetitions of the modeling display. Finally, imitation will be more likely if the viewer is encouraged to rehearse or practice what he or she has seen. In short, repetitive watching of a rewarded model of the viewer's age and sex, and rehearsing the observed behaviors, will increase the amount of imitation that occurs.

Conformity Pressure

People with problems often have problems with people. Clients often seek help in the first place because of difficulty in getting along with others, and this difficulty can be reflected in low attraction (dislike, suspiciousness, ambivalence) toward the therapist. Under such circumstances, attempts to increase attraction by telling (structuring), negotiating (meanings), or showing (imitation) the client appropriate materials may not succeed. Use of conformity pressure is another alternative. In the typical use of conformity pressure in the research laboratory, a group of individuals meet, and each member in turn is required to make a judgment aloud—about which of two lines is longer, whether a dot of light moved, which social or political viewpoint is best, and so on. However, unknown to one member of the group (the subject), all the other members are actually accomplices of the group leader and are told in advance to respond to the subject's requests for their judgments in a predetermined and usually unanimous or nearly unanimous manner. In at least a third of these groups, the subject conforms to the majority judgment, even when it is, to an outsider, obviously incorrect. Research conducted in counseling settings indicates that conformity pressure can indeed serve as a powerful attraction enhancer (Goldstein, 1971). After hearing a taped session between a helper and client, three members (accomplices) of a group of four "clients" rated the helper aloud as being attractive in a variety of ways. The real client conformed to this pressure and did likewise. In other groups, different real clients also rated the taped helper as highly attractive after conformity pressure from accomplices, even when the helper being rated was, again, to outside observers highly unattractive in several important respects.

Therapist Expertness and Status

The therapeutic relationship emphasizes reciprocal liking, respect, and trust. Seeking to improve the relationship by focusing on attraction enhancement is equivalent to emphasizing the liking component of this relationship. Relationships can also be enhanced by procedures relevant to the respect component. A major means of enhancing client respect for the helper concerns the helper's real or apparent expertness and status. In general, the greater the helper's expertness, the greater the client's respect.

In psychotherapy, there is much about the psychotherapist, and his or her behavior and physical surroundings, that testifies to expertness and authority. Haley (1963) has commented in this regard:

> The context of the relationship emphasizes the therapist's position. . . . Patients are usually referred to him by people who point out what a capable authority he is and how much the patient needs help. Some therapists have a waiting list, so that the patient is impressed by standing in line to be treated, while others may imply that patients with similar symptoms were successfully treated. Furthermore, the patient must be willing to pay money even to talk to the therapist, and the therapist can either treat him or dismiss him, and so controls whether or not there is going to be a relationship. Not only the therapist's prestige is emphasized in the initial meeting, but also the patient's inadequacy is made clear. The patient . . . must emphasize his difficulties in life to a man who apparently has none. The physical settings in which most therapists function also reinforce their superior position. In many instances the therapist sits at a desk, the symbol of authority, while the patient sits in a chair, the position of the suppliant. In psychoanalytic therapy the arrangement is more

extreme. The patient lies down while the therapist sits up. His chair is also placed so that he can observe the patient's reactions, but the patient cannot observe him. Finally, the initial interview in therapy usually makes quite explicit the fact that the therapist is in charge of the relationship by the rules for treatment he lays down. He suggests the frequency of interviews, implies he will be the one who decides when treatment will end, and he usually instructs the patient how to behave in the office. He may make a general statement about how the patient is to express himself there, or he may provide specific instructions as in the analytic situation where the patient is told he must lie down and say whatever comes to mind.

What else is there that distinguishes the expert from the inexpert therapist? Research reported by Schmidt and Strong (1970) has shown that to a large extent clients judge expertness by the observable behavior of the therapist. According to these investigators' results, college students describe the expert and inexpert counselor quite differently:

The *expert* shakes the student's hand, aligning the student with himself, and greets him with his first name. He seems interested and relaxed. He has a neat appearance but is not stuffy. . . . He talks at the student's level and is not arrogant toward him. The expert assumes a comfortable but attentive sitting position. He focuses his attention on the student and carefully listens to him. He has a warm facial expression and is reactive to the student. His voice is inflective and lively, he changes his facial expressions, and uses hand gestures. He speaks fluently with confidence and sureness. The expert has prepared for the interview. He is informed as to why the student is there and is familiar with the student's test scores, grades, and background. . . . He asks direct and to-the-point questions. His questions are thought-provoking and follow an apparently logical progression. They seem spontaneous and conversational. The expert is willing to help determine if the student's decisions are right, but does not try to change the student's ideas forcefully. He lets the student do most of the talking and does not interrupt him. The expert moves quickly to the root of the problem. He points out contradictions in reasoning, and restates the student's statements as they bear on the problem. . . . He makes recommendations and suggests possible solutions.

The *inexpert* is awkward, tense, and uneasy. He seems to be afraid of the student. He does not greet the student by name to put him at ease. . . . He is not quite sure of himself or of some of his remarks. He seems too cold, strict and dominating, and too formal in attitude and action. His gestures are stiff and overdone. . . . The inexpert slouches in his chair. He is too casual and relaxed. . . . His voice is flat and without inflection, appearing to show disinterest and boredom. . . . The inexpert comes to the interview cold. He has not cared enough about the student to acquaint himself with the student's records. The inexpert asks vague questions which are trivial and irrelevant and have no common thread or aim. His questioning is abrupt and tactless with poor transitions. He asks too many questions like a quiz session, giving the student the third degree. . . . The inexpert is slow in getting his point across and is confusing in his discussion of what the student should do. . . . The inexpert does not get to the core of the problem. . . . He just doesn't seem to be getting anywhere. (Schmidt & Strong, 1970, p. 117)

These descriptions were then used as the script outline in a study examining the effects of status on therapists' influence. Counselors taking the role of expert and inexpert were thoroughly rehearsed in the aforementioned behaviors. The former were introduced to clients with the following statement:

The person you will be talking with is Dr. _____ , a psychologist who has had several years of experience interviewing students. (p.83)

The inexpert helper was, by contrast, introduced with this statement:

We had originally scheduled Dr. _____ to talk with you, but unfortunately he notified us that he wouldn't

be able to make it today. In his place we have
Mr. _____ , a student who unfortunately has had no
interviewing experience and has been given only a
brief explanation of the purpose of this study. I think
he should work out all right, though. (p. 83)

Analysis of therapist-client interviews revealed, as predicted, greater positive change in those clients structured and in fact seen by the "expert" helper.

It thus seems that the greater the change agent's expertness, the greater his or her effectiveness in altering the behavior and beliefs of the target individual. Laboratory research strongly supports this contention. A number of investigations confirm that a statement is more fully accepted and acted on when the recipient believes it comes from an expert or high-status person than when its apparent source is a person of low or unknown expertness.

The first evidence obtained by my own research group of the relationship aspect of this finding was almost accidental (Goldstein, 1971). We conducted a study with the purpose of determining whether client attraction to the therapist would increase if the helper went out of his way to do a small favor or extend an extra courtesy to the client. The courtesy involved was offering the client coffee and a doughnut, not an unusual event in counseling or psychotherapy. Although this procedure did improve the relationship, attraction increased even more when the helper made it clear that the coffee and doughnut were for himself and not for the client! We had not predicted this result and only half-jokingly speculated that perhaps attraction increased because of client belief that anyone behaving so boorishly must be an important person. In other words, perhaps attraction increased because, in the client's eyes, the therapist had increased his status.

This issue was tested more directly in a subsequent investigation (Sabalis, 1969). Sabalis had four groups of clients, two of whom were seen by what appeared to be a high-status helper, two by a low-status helper. Not all persons, Sabalis predicted, are attracted to high-status helpers. Authoritarian persons—those rigidly respectful of authority—seem to be highly responsive and attracted to such individuals, whereas more equalitarian persons are less drawn to them. The study then tested the hypothesis that a high-status therapist would increase the attraction-to-helper of authoritarian clients but not of equalitarian clients.

Clients (of both kinds) in the high-status groups each received a postcard indicating the time of the interview. The interviewer was "Dr. Robert Sabalis." When each client arrived for the interview, the interviewer introduced himself as "Dr. Sabalis, a member of the faculty of the psychology department." A "Dr. Robert Sabalis" nameplate was on the interviewer's desk, and the office itself was a large, well-furnished one belonging to a faculty member. The interviewer was neatly dressed in a business suit. The session began with some test taking by the client. The interviewer described the tests as being ones on which he was doing research. As the client filled out the test forms, the interviewer opened a text and began to jot down notes from it, indicating to the client as he did that he was preparing an examination for one of the classes he taught.

For the low-status groups, the interviewer's name on the postcard and in his introduction on meeting was "Bob Sabalis." He described himself to clients as a senior undergraduate psychology major who was meeting with them as a requirement for one of his own courses. His attire was consistent with the typical undergraduate's. The interview office was quite small and sparsely furnished. As the test taking commenced, he again began note taking from a text, but this time he indicated he was preparing for an examination he had to take.

The predicted effect of status on attraction was obtained. That is, highly authoritarian clients became significantly more attracted to the interviewer after the high-status, but not the low-status, procedures.

As described earlier, Schmidt and Strong (1970) showed the positive effect of expertness by training counselors to behave as either expert or inexpert. Sabalis used one interviewer, who served as both the high- and the low-status therapist. The positive effect on the therapist-client relationship was obtained again. Similar findings have been reported by other researchers (Atkinson & Carskeddon, 1975; Dell & Schmidt, 1976; Greenberg, 1969; Kerr, Olson, Claiborn, Bauers-Gruenler, & Paolo, 1983; Spiegel, 1976). Corrigan, Dell, Lewis, and Schmidt (1980) have provided a comprehensive review of these studies, examining the array of evidential, reputational, and behavioral cues to therapist expertness and status that have been shown with reliability to have attraction-enhancing potency. While limitations on the generality of this find-ing may exist as a function of the degree to which the client per-ceives his or her therapist to be a central or peripheral concern (Petty & Cacioppo, 1981; Petty & Wegener, 1998), it is nonetheless largely the case that therapist expertness and status serve to increase client respect, which in turn leads to the client's being more open to the therapist's attempts to influence him or her and, subsequently, greater likelihood of client change.

Therapist Empathy

The level of empathy offered by the therapist and the effects of empathy on the client have been the object of considerable the-ory and research. This research has consistently shown that a therapist's empathy with the client's feelings strongly influences the quality of the therapist-client relationship that develops and, at least with a substantial proportion of clients, the degree of client change.

Truax and Carkhuff (1967) have been quite active in studying the effects of empathy on the therapist-client relationship. They have commented in the following way with regard to empathy:

> As we come to know some of [the client's] wants, some
> of his needs, some of his achievements and some of his
> failures, we find ourselves as therapists "living" with the
> patient much as we do with the central figure of a
> novel. . . . Just as with the character in the novel, we
> come to know the person from his own internal frame
> of reference, gaining some flavor of his moment-by-
> moment experience. We see events and significant peo-
> ple in his life as they appear to him—not as they
> "objectively are" but as he experiences them. As we
> come to know him from his personal vantage point we
> automatically come to value and like him. . . . We
> begin to perceive the events and experiences of his life
> "as if" they were parts of our own life. It is through this
> process that we come to feel warmth, respect and lik-
> ing. (p. 42)

As a means of reliably rating the degree of empathy offered by the therapist to the client, these same researchers developed the widely used scale shown in Table 3.1.

TABLE 3.1
Empathic Understanding in Interpersonal Processes

LEVEL 1

The verbal and behavioral expressions of the helper either do not attend to or detract significantly from the verbal and behavioral expressions of the client(s) in that they communicate significantly less of the client's feelings and experiences than the client has communicated himself.

> *Example:* The helper communicates no awareness of even the most obvious, expressed surface feelings of the client. The helper may be bored or disinterested or simply operating from a preconceived frame of reference which totally excludes that of the client(s).

In summary, the helper does everything but express that he is listening, understanding, or being sensitive to even the most obvious feelings of the client in such a way as to detract significantly from the communications of the client.

LEVEL 2

While the helper responds to the expressed feelings of the client(s), he does so in such a way that he subtracts noticeable affect from the communications of the client.

> *Example:* The helper may communicate some awareness of obvious, surface feelings of the client, but his communications drain off a level of the affect and distort the level of meaning. The helper may communicate his own ideas of what may be going on, but these are not congruent with the expressions of the client.

In summary, the helper tends to respond to other than what the client is expressing or indicating.

LEVEL 3

The expressions of the helper in response to the expressions of the client(s) are essentially interchangeable with those of the client in that they express essentially the same affect and meaning.

> *Example:* The helper responds with accurate understandings of the surface feelings of the client but may not respond to or may misinterpret the deeper feelings.

In summary, the helper is responding so as to neither subtract from nor add to the expressions of the client. He does not respond accurately to how that person really feels beneath the surface feelings; but he indicates a willingness and openness to do so. Level 3 constitutes the minimal level of facilitative interpersonal functioning.

LEVEL 4

The responses of the helper add noticeably to the expressions of the client(s) in such a way as to express feelings a level deeper than the client was able to express himself.

Example: The helper communicates his understanding of the expressions of the client at a level deeper than they were expressed and thus enables the client to experience and/or express feelings he was unable to express previously.

In summary, the helper's responses add deeper feeling and meaning to the expression of the client.

LEVEL 5

The helper's responses add significantly to the feeling and meaning of the expressions of the client(s) in such a way as to accurately express feelings levels below what the client himself was able to express or, in the event of ongoing, deep self-exploration on the client's part, to be fully with him in his deepest moments.

Example: The helper responds with accuracy to all of the client's deeper as well as surface feelings. He is "tuned in" on the client's wave length. The helper and the client might proceed together to explore previously unexplored areas of human existence.

In summary, the helper is responding with a full awareness of who the other person is and with a comprehensive and accurate empathic understanding of that individual's deepest feelings.

Note. From *Toward Effective Counseling and Therapy* (pp. 174–175) by C. B. Truax and R. R. Carkhuff, 1967, Chicago: Aldine de Gruyter. Reprinted by permission.

A great deal of research has been done on the effects of high levels of therapist empathy in counseling, guidance, and psychotherapy. Certain effects on the client regularly occur in these studies. Feeling understood, that someone has been able to truly perceive his or her deeper feelings, increases the client's liking of the helper. In a sense, the client also comes to trust himself or herself more under these circumstances, for one regular result of a high level of helper empathy is deeper and more persevering self-exploration by the client. In several of these studies, greater client change is a clear result.

A more concrete understanding of helper empathy and its effects on client behavior is provided by the example that follows, drawn from a psychotherapy session.* Note how all helper statements are at least Level 3, and often higher.

Helpee: Um. I don't know whether, whether I'm right or wrong in feeling the way I do, but, uh, I find myself withdrawing from people. I don't care to go out and socialize and play their stupid little games any more. Um, I get very anxious and come home depressed and have headaches—it seems all so superficial. There was a time when I used to get along with everybody, everybody said, "Oh, isn't she wonderful! She gets along with everybody; she's so nice and everybody likes her," and I used to think that was . . . that was something to be really proud of, but, oh, but, I think that only told how I, or who I was at that time, that I had no depth. I was sort of whatever the crowd wanted me to be, or the particular group I was with at the time. Um, I know it's important for my husband's business that we go out and socialize and meet people and make a good impression and join clubs and play all those stupid little games—Elks, and, you know, bowling banquets, and, uh, fishing trips and fraternity-type gatherings. Um, I . . . I just don't care to do it any more, and, um, I don't know if that means that I'm a . . . that there's something wrong with me psychologically, or uh, or is this normal. I mean . . . uh . . . people don't really know who I am and they really don't care who one another, who the other person is. They . . . it's all at such a superficial level.

Helper: You're darn sure of how you feel, but you really don't know what it all adds up to. Is it you? Is it the other people? What are the implications of your husband's business? You? Where is it all going?

Helpee: Uh-huh. It's an empty life. It's, um, there's, uh, no depth to it at all. I mean, you just talk about very, very superficial things, and the first few times, it's OK. But then after that, there's nothing to talk about. So you drink and you pretend to be happy over silly jokes and

---

*From *Helping and Human Relations* (pp. 219–220) by R. R. Carkhuff, 1969, New York: Holt, Rinehart and Winston. Reprinted by permission.

silly things that people do when they all, uh, are trying to impress one another, and they're very materialistic, and, uh, it's just not the route I want to go.

Helper: So your feelings are so strong now that you just can't fake it any more.

Helpee: That's right, so what do you do? People say, "Oh, there's something wrong with you," then, "You need to see a psychiatrist or something," because you . . . you know the thing in society is that the normal person gets along with people, and uh, can adjust to any situation. And when you . . . when you're a little discriminating, maybe very discriminating or critical, then that means there's something wrong with you.

Helper: While you know how strongly you feel about all these things, you're not sure you can really act in terms of them and be free.

Helpee: I don't know if I'm strong enough. The implications are great. It may mean, uh, a breakup of the marriage, uh, and it means going it alone, and that's too frightening. I don't think I have the courage. But I do feel like I'm in sort of a trap.

Helper: You know you can't pretend, yet you're really fearful of going it alone.

Helpee: Yes, there's nobody I can really talk to, I mean, you know, it's one thing if you have a . . . like your husband . . . if you can share these things, if he can understand it at some level, but . . . um . . . he can't.

Helper: It's like, "If I act on how I really feel, though, it frightens the people who mean most to me. They won't understand it, and I sure can't share that with them."

Helpee: *(Pause)* So what do you do. *(Pause)* I mean . . . I . . . you know. I find myself going out and telling the people who I really feel about, about different topics and getting into controversial issues, and, uh, and that's, that's too anxiety provoking for me. I can't, because then you get into arguments and I don't want to do that either, that leads nowhere. I just get frustrated and anxious and upset and angry with myself for getting myself into the situation.

Helper: You know that doesn't set you free, you know . . .

Helpee: No, it bottles me up.

Helper: That only causes you more problems, and what you're really asking about is, how you can move toward greater freedom and greater fulfillment in your own life.

Helpee: I . . . I think I know who I am now, independent of other people, and, uh, which people aren't and . . . um . . . there's no room for that kind of person in this society.

Helper: There's no room for me out there!

Helpee: *(Pause)* So what do I do?

Helper: We run over and over the questions that . . . you end up with. "Where do I go from here? How do I act on this? I know how I feel, but I don't know what'll happen if I act on how I feel."

Helpee: I . . . have an idea of what'll happen.

Helper: And it's not good!

Helpee: No! It means almost starting a whole new life.

Helper: And you don't know if you can make it.

Helpee: Right, I know what I've got here, and if I don't make it all the way with the other, then I'm in trouble.

Helper: While you don't know what'll happen if you act on your feelings, you know what the alternatives are if you don't. And they're not good either. They're worse.

Helpee: I . . . I don't have much choice.

Carkhuff (1969) has provided the following guidelines for helpers wishing to become proficient in offering clients a high level of empathic response. Helpers will find they are most effective in communicating an empathic understanding when they are doing as follows:

1. Concentrating with intensity upon the client's expressions, both verbal and nonverbal

2. Concentrating upon responses that are interchangeable with those of the client (Level 3)

3. Formulating responses in language that is most attuned to the client

4. Responding in a feeling tone similar to that communicated by the client

5. Being most responsive

6. Having established an interchangeable base of communication (Level 3), moving tentatively toward expanding and clarifying the client's experiences at higher levels (Levels 4 and 5)

7. Concentrating upon what is not being expressed by the client, and, in a sense, seeking to fill in what is missing rather than simply dealing with what is present

8. Employing the client's behavior as the best guideline to assess the effectiveness of their responses

Programs for training therapists and other change agents to develop and communicate empathy have been offered by Egan (1976), Guerney (1977), and Ivey and Authier (1971), as well as by myself and colleagues (Goldstein & Michaels, 1985). Our approach rests on a multicomponent definition of the empathic process provided by Keefe (1976). He suggests that the first phase of the empathic sequence begins as the therapist perceives the feeling state and thoughts of the client. In the second phase, the therapist's perceptions generate both cognitive and affective responses in himself or herself. Here, consistent with Reik's (1949) notion of reverberation, the therapist seeks to avoid categorization, value judgments, hypotheses, or other cognitive analysis. Instead, such processes are held in abeyance while he or she allows and encourages a largely unfettered, "as-if" experience of the client's affective world. In the next phase, that of detachment and decoding, the therapist labels the feelings he or she has sought to experience (i.e., those perceived as being experienced by the client). Once feelings have been perceived, reverberated, and labeled, the therapist communicates accurate feedback (e.g., Levels 3, 4, 5 of the Truax and Carkhuff scale) to the target person as the final phase of the empathic sequence.

To bring therapists and other change agents to high levels of competence in the development and communication of empathy, defined in terms of Keefe's (1976) components, we have prepared the following training program (Goldstein, 1999).

Readiness Training

An optimal empathy training program, in our view, commences with training activities designed to maximize the likelihood that the trainee will be fully prepared to understand, acquire, and use the four skills that constitute empathy (perceive, reverberate, label, communicate). Such preparatory training would ideally take two complementary forms. The first concerns efforts to help the trainee acquire a series of what might be termed *empathy-preparatory* skills (i.e., abilities potentiating empathy skills acquisition). Frank (1977) has developed and evaluated just such a readiness program. In it, trainees were successfully taught (a) imagination skills, which significantly increased accurate identification of implied meanings; (b) behavioral observation skills, which significantly increased accurate predictions of other persons' overt behavior; and (c) flexibility skills (in shifting from *a* to *b*), which significantly increased the use of differentiated levels of social reasoning.

It is likely that training in the perceptual, affective reverberation, cognitive analysis, and communication skills will be enhanced not only by preparatory skills such as those offered by Frank (1977), but also by the reduction or elimination of what might be termed *empathy skill-acquisition inhibitors*. Bullmer's (1972) programmed self-instructional approach to training the perceptual component of empathy contains at least one such inhibition-reduction component (i.e., the effort to help trainees understand and ameliorate the influence of perceptual biases and certain types of implicit interpersonal theorizing). Pereira (1978) contributed a second such effort in his use of Interpersonal Process Recall (Kagan, 1972), not to teach aspects of empathy per se but to reduce "affect-associated anxiety," making trainee approach to such affects more possible. Clearly, the role of training in readiness skills and reduction of empathy inhibitors in potentiating empathy skill is a valuable subject for future empirical efforts.

Perceptual Training

As noted earlier, Keefe (1976) proposed that empathy commences with the perception of the other person, as the empathizer nonevaluatively observes and records an array of verbal and nonverbal behaviors, physical characteristics, environmental attributes, and other aspects of the ongoing interpersonal context. I agree with this perspective and propose that, for optimal empathy training, the readiness stage be followed by purposeful perceptual training. The existing training technology is not large, but promising possibilities do exist. One is the programmed self-instructional approach developed by Bullmer (1972). As discussed, the thrust of Bullmer's materials is the training of more accurate, less distorted, less inferential, and more objective perception.

A second promising approach to enhancing perceptual accuracy in interpersonal contexts is described by Henry Smith in his books *Sensitivity Training* (Smith, 1973) and *Sensitivity to People* (Smith, 1966). As I have done with empathy, Smith takes a components perspective to sensitivity. He does so to enhance training effectiveness:

> Should we take a general or components view of sensitivity? The answer depends, in part, on whether the purpose is to select sensitive people or to train them. If selection is the aim, then the general answer is to be favored. What we wish in selection is to place individuals on a single scale that ranges from the least to the most sensitive. If training is the aim, however, then a components view is very helpful. Viewing sensitivity as a general ability gives us no clues as to where to begin training, what to train for, or how to train. (Smith, 1973, p. 23)

To be sure, sensitivity, like empathy, is in the real world expressed as a gestalt, not as individual components. A components view, though in this sense artificial, is heuristically superior in the functional sense of utility for training. As with programmed instruction, the pieces may be learned first and then sequentially combined to form the whole.

The first component of Smith's concept of sensitivity (i.e., "observational sensitivity") is identical to the perceptual accuracy component of empathy in Keefe's (1976) and my own definitions of the concept. Smith (1973) states:

> We define and shall use observational sensitivity in a specific way as the ability to look at and listen to another person and remember what he looked like and said. Observation is sometimes pictured as a quite passive affair: the eye is a motion-picture camera; the ear, a tape recorder. What we see a person do and hear him say is transcribed on the slate of our awareness.

The records are then sorted, edited, and evaluated. No picture could be further from the truth, for we do not observe people; we perceive them. And we perceive what we want to perceive, what we expect to perceive, and what we have learned to perceive. Perceivers differ widely in their ability to discriminate what they see and hear from what they feel and infer about a person. It is an important task of training to develop the ability to make such discriminations. (p. 24)

Accordingly, Smith (1973) distinguishes between sensory impressions, the enhancement of which is the goal of perceptual accuracy training, and expressive impressions, which interfere with perceptual accuracy. The goal of Smith's observational sensitivity training—my own perceptual accuracy training—is to increase trainee competence in recording sensory impressions (what the other person looked like, said, and did) and in discriminating these observations from inferential, derivative, and interpretive expressive impressions (the other's feelings, beliefs, motivations, and traits). Smith (1973) describes the process of becoming a sensitive observer in the following way:

To become a good observer, the trainee must learn to shift his attention from the subjective to the objective, from himself to the other person. (p. 78)

The goal of observational training should be to develop the trainee's ability to discriminate sensory from expressive qualities. The critical problem in observational training is not that we make poor observations that lead to faulty inferences; it is that we do not make observations or inferences at all. We do not merely see or hear a person, we perceive a quality in the person. . . . We do not see a redhead and hear a loud voice; we perceive an "interesting," "intelligent," and "level-headed" person or one who is "narrow-minded," "irritating," and "insincere." (p. 242)

How is this training goal to be achieved? Smith (1973) proposes that observational sensitivity training might be responsive to the apparent difficulties that individuals have in maintaining objectivity in anxiety-arousing interpersonal contexts: "*The* problem of observational training is to teach trainees to maintain the observer role in tense interpersonal situations. It is then that the perception of sensory qualities intensify" (p. 79).

Perhaps, then, participants in observational sensitivity training ought to be exposed to progressively more intense levels of interpersonal stress and even confrontation while trainers prompt them to keep their focus on the other's objective qualities, not on the other's inferred characteristics or participants' internal reactions. Such a training effort, Smith (1973) suggests, might make use of the affect stimulation films developed by Kagan and Schauble (1969). In these films, the speaker addresses the viewer with progressively heightened negative affect: rejection, hostility, and so on. The trainee's task in the face of such escalating affect is to continue to report what the person in the film looked like, said, and did. Smith suggests that interpersonal stress levels could be heightened further through simulated interactions with real-life, face-to-face implementations of the hierarchical training strategy. While Smith's proposal for effective observational sensitivity training has not yet received extensive empirical scrutiny, an initial examination of its value by Danish and Brodsky (1970) has been clearly encouraging.

Affective Reverberation Training

An extended series of procedures for affective reverberation training are available. These include meditation (Goleman, 1977; Lesh, 1970; Maupin, 1965, 1972); structural integration or Rolfing (Johnson, 1977; Keen, 1970; Rolf, 1977); Reichian therapy (Baker, 1967; Lowen, 1975; Reich, 1933/1951); bioenergetics (Lowen & Lowen, 1977); the Alexander technique (Alexander, 1969); Feldenkrais' Awareness through Movement (Feldenkrais, 1970, 1972); dance therapy (Bernstein, 1975; Davis, 1973; Pesso, 1969); sensory awareness training (Brooks, 1974; Guenther, 1968; Selver, 1957); focusing (Gendlin, 1981, 1984); and the Laban-Bartenieff multilevel method (Bartenieff & Lewis, 1980; Laban & Lawrence, 1947). All these somatapsychic methods, oriented toward enhancing affective reverberation (and, in some instances, also perceptual accuracy), have been at best at the fringes of scientific psychology. Yet that is precisely where some of psychology's most profound and most effective interventions have begun—in the wisdom and experience of creative clinicians. Whether some or any of these techniques, and which ones, will prove on experimental scrutiny to be of value for teaching the affective reverberation component of empathy are empirical questions worthy of examination.

Cognitive Analysis Training

From a components perspective on empathy, following perception (i.e., the nonevaluative recording of the other's behavior) and affective reverberation (i.e., the trying-on, "as-if" experiencing of the other's affects), the observer steps back from the other's behavior and his or her own reverberatory experience to discern the nature of and label the other's affects. Training for high levels of competence in this stage of cognitive analysis is optimally provided by the Carkhuff's (1969) discrimination training procedures. Such discrimination training rests on a reasonably firm foundation of evaluative evidence, has been adapted for diverse trainee populations, and has been shown to be a prerequisite for adequate skill at the final, communicative stage of empathy.

Beyond Carkhuff's (1969) discrimination training method and materials, additional techniques of possible value for cognitive analysis enhancement exist. A number of studies suggest that combining exposure to different facial expressions and guided practice and feedback regarding the accuracy of affective labeling of the expressions (i.e., cognitive analysis) is effective in enhancing accuracy of judgments (Berlin, 1974; Healy, 1973; Lopez, 1977). Readers interested in pursuing this ancillary means for the enhancement of the cognitive analysis phase of empathy will find ample experimental materials for doing so in the creative work put forth by the research groups of Ekman (1965, 1972) and Rosenthal (Rosenthal, 1966; Rosenthal & DePaulo, 1979).

Communication

Earlier in this chapter, I described aspects of the Truax and Carkhuff (1967) approach to empathy training and referred briefly to some similarly targeted conditional approaches. The training methods thus used typically include instructions, modeling (an especially popular empathy-training technique), role-playing or behavioral rehearsal, and some form of systematic feedback. The experiential component of these training programs, when offered, typically has been a combination of supervised experience conducting actual counseling sessions and a group experience of a sensitivity-training or quasitherapeutic type (Egan, 1976; Goldstein, 1973; Guerney, 1977; Ivey & Authier, 1971; Truax & Carkhuff, 1967).

Transfer and Maintenance Training

It has been demonstrated in the context of psychotherapy that gains made by patients during the course of treatment fail in the majority of instances to manifest themselves either outside the treatment setting (a failure of transfer, or generalization over settings) or over time (a failure of maintenance, or generalization over time; Goldstein & Martens, 2000; Goldstein & Kanfer, 1979; Kazdin, 1975; Keeley, Shemberg, & Carbonell, 1976). Many observers have held that poor transfer and maintenance of therapeutic gain are the most telling weaknesses of contemporary psychotherapy. The paucity of follow-up studies on the transfer and maintenance of empathic skill after training, and the essentially negative outcome of the few studies that do exist (e.g., Collingswood, 1971; Gantt, Billingsley, & Giordano, 1980; Guzzetta, 1974) suggest that a similarly dismal postintervention picture exists for such training. This is the bad news. The good news, however, is that many emerging techniques do exist with the explicit goal of enhancing transfer and maintenance. Furthermore, a fair amount of outcome evidence already demonstrates the efficacy of these techniques in a psychotherapeutic context and, in at least a few instances, in the context of empathy training (Bath, 1976; Collingswood, 1971; Guzzetta, 1974; Jones, 1974; Rocks, Baker, & Guerney, 1982). Enhancement techniques with a long history of efficacy in other domains of psychological intervention and with preliminary demonstrable effectiveness in skills-training contexts are as follows:

1. *Provision of general principles:* Being given the rules, strategies, or organizing principles that govern skill performance in the training and application settings

2. *Maximizing identical elements:* Building high levels of similarity in the interpersonal and/or physical qualities of the training and application settings

3. *Overlearning:* Ensuring that the trainee practices correct skill behaviors a number of times after the initial correct demonstration

4. *Stimulus variability:* Arranging for the trainee to train with different persons and in different contexts when engaging in trials for overlearning skill use

5. *Self-regulation:* Teaching the trainee the skills necessary to monitor, reward, and punish his or her own skill use in real-world settings

6. *Promotive environments:* Teaching the trainee's real-world significant others (e.g., parents, peers) procedures for monitoring, rewarding, and punishing trainee skill use in real-world settings

Therapist empathy appears to be a vital piece of any efforts to enhance therapist-client relationships. Its training is elaborate but, I propose, likely to be well worth the effort.

Therapist Warmth

As is true for empathy, therapist warmth is a central ingredient of the helping relationship. Whatever specific change methods the therapist uses, their likelihood of success is largely a result of the relationship base on which therapist and client interact. Therapist warmth is a very important aspect of this base. Without it, specific helping procedures can be technically correct but therapeutically impotent.

Therapist warmth is also important in the therapeutic relationship because it appears to beget reciprocal warmth from the client. Truax and Carkhuff (1967), in fact, have commented that "It is a rare human being who does not respond to warmth with warmth and to hostility with hostility. It is probably the most important principle for the beginning therapist to understand if he is to be successful in the therapeutic relationship" (p. 127). This contention has received ample support in the research program described earlier in this chapter (Goldstein, 1971). When liking of A for B (helper for client) was increased by structuring, status enhancement, or other procedures, B's liking of A reciprocally increased—even though no procedures whatsoever had been applied to B. Several other researchers have reported the same reciprocal result. The Truax and Carkhuff definition of this therapist quality, and their examples of its occurrence in counseling and psychotherapy, help clarify the nature and significance of therapist warmth:

> The dimension of nonpossessive warmth or unconditional positive regard ranges from a high level, where the therapist warmly accepts the patient's experience as part of that person without imposing conditions, to a low level, where the therapist evaluates a patient or his or her feelings, expresses dislike or disapproval, or expresses warmth in a selective and evaluative way.

> *Level 1.* The therapist is actively offering advice or giving clear negative regard. He or she could be telling the patient what would be "best" for him or her, or in other ways actively approving or disapproving of his or her behavior. The therapist's actions make him or her the locus of evaluation; he or she sees himself or herself as responsible for the patient.

> *Level 2.* The therapist responds mechanically to the client, indicating little positive regard and hence little nonpossessive warmth. He or she might ignore the patient or his or her feelings or display a lack of concern or interest. The therapist ignores the client at times when a nonpossessively warm response would be expected; he or she shows a complete passivity that communicates almost unconditional lack of regard.

> *Level 3.* The therapist indicates a positive caring for the patient or client, but it is a semipossessive caring in the sense that she or he communicates to the client that her or his behavior matters to the therapist. That is, the therapist communicates such things as "It is not all right if you act immorally," "I want you to get along at work," or "It's important to me that you get along with the ward staff." The therapist sees herself or himself as responsible for the client.

> *Level 4.* The therapist clearly communicates a very deep interest and concern for the welfare of the patient, showing a nonevaluative and unconditional warmth in

almost all areas of functioning. Although there remains
some conditionality in the more personal and private
areas, the patient is given freedom to be himself or herself and to be liked as himself or herself. There is little
evaluation of thoughts and behaviors. In deeply personal areas, however, the therapist might be conditional
and communicate the idea that the client may act in
any way he or she wishes—except that it is important
to the therapist that he or she be more mature, or not
regress in therapy, or accept and like the therapist. In
all other areas, however, nonpossessive warmth is communicated. The therapist sees himself or herself as
responsible to the client.

Level 5. At Level 5, the therapist communicates warmth
without restriction. There is a deep respect for the
patient's worth as a person and his or her rights as a
free individual. At this level the patient is free to be
himself or herself even if this means that he or she is
regressing, being defensive, or even disliking or rejecting the therapist. At this stage the therapist cares deeply
for the patient as a person, but it does not matter to
him or her how the patient chooses to behave. The
therapist genuinely cares for and deeply prizes the
patient for his or her human potentials, apart from evaluations of his or her behavior or thoughts. The therapist is willing to share equally the patient's joys and
aspirations or depressions and failures. The only chan-
neling by the therapist might be the demand that the
patient communicate personally relevant material.
(Truax & Carkhuff, 1967, pp. 58–68)

Raush and Bordin (1957) define therapist warmth further, as
a function of three components:

Commitment. The therapist most typically commits a
specified amount of time to the patient; he commits, for
the patient's use at those times, a private meeting place
which will remain relatively undisturbed by extraneous
factors; he commits his skills and his efforts at understanding and aiding the patient; he also commits to the
patient a relationship in which the patient's needs and

interests are dominant, and in which the therapist's personal demands are minimized.

Effort to understand. The therapist shows his effort to understand by asking questions designed to elicit the patient's view of himself and the world, by testing with the patient the impressions that he, the therapist, has gained of these views, and by indicating, by comments or other forms of action, his interest in understanding the patient's views. . . . Certainly, it is the therapist's efforts at understanding which produce the first major emotional tie between patient and therapist in most forms of psychotherapy. . . . Such an effort on the part of the therapist may be communicated in many ways: by attentive and unintrusive listening, by questions indicative of interest, by sounds of encouragement, by any of the verbal or nonverbal cues which say in effect, "I am interested in what you are saying and feeling—go on." But whatever the manner of communication, the effort at understanding on the part of the therapist is communication of warmth.

Spontaneity. "Simply going through the motions of psychotherapy is not enough," is, and must be, emphasized by supervisors of students of the process. The therapist must be capable of expressing something of himself. . . . Observation of different therapists indicates considerable variability in the amount of affect expressed. Some therapists seems always to have a tight rein on themselves; they are or seem to be emotionless.

Others seem to feel much freer to express themselves; they seem more "natural." (Raush & Bordin, 1957, p. 352)

Similar behaviors represent warmth in yet other research. In one, during the warm interview the interviewer smiled, nodded her head, and spoke warmly. During the cold interview she spoke without smiling, did not nod her head, and kept her voice drab and cold (Simonson, 1968). As in much of this type of research, interviewees talked significantly more to the warm interviewer. Another study with a similar result used speaking in a soft, melodic, and pleasant voice versus speaking in a harsh, impersonal, and businesslike voice for the comparison of warm versus cold therapists (Morris & Suckerman, 1974a). In a successful replication (Morris & Suckerman, 1974b), the same researchers elaborated their definition of warmth in a manner akin to Raush and Bordin's constructions of commitment and effort to understand. Specifically, in addition to varying the voice quality, the warm therapist showed interest, concern, and attention, whereas the cold therapist displayed a lack of interest, concern, and attentiveness.

Though it is clear that therapists can be trained to reliably show warmth, and that therapist warmth has been shown to affect what the client does, readers must be cautioned against too rigid adoption of a "warm stance." Smiling, a pleasant voice, and the like can indeed represent warmth. But if at root warmth is, as Raush and Bordin have suggested, commitment, effort to understand, and spontaneity, warmth can also be represented behaviorally by directiveness, assertiveness, autonomy-enhancing distancing, and even anger. Largely, it is the context and content of the therapist-client interaction that will determine whether or not a given instance of helper behavior is perceived by the client as warm.

Additional Procedures

The bulk of both research and theory regarding means for enhancing the therapist-client relationship has focused on these approaches: structuring (both client and therapist); negotiation of meaning; imitation; and therapist expertness, empathy, and warmth. Other, less fully examined or developed procedures for relationship enhancement have also been identified and are briefly described in the following pages to encourage further inquiry into their utility.

Helper-Client Matching

This approach to the helping relationship, in contrast with those just considered, typically does not seek to alter anything in the helper or client in order to enhance the "goodness" of their fit. Instead, an effort is made to (a) identify real characteristics of helpers and clients that are relevant to how well they relate, (b) measure helpers and clients on these characteristics, and (c) match helpers and clients into pairs optimal for client change on the basis of these measurements. Much of the research on matching is conflicting or inconclusive, but some of it does lead to useful, if tentative, conclusions. Following are characteristics of an optimal helper-client match.

1. Helper and client hold congruent expectations of the role each is to play in the relationship. They understand and agree on their respective rights and obligations regarding what each is expected to do and not to do during their inter- actions.

2. Helper and client are both confident of positive results from their meetings. Each anticipates at least a reasonably high likelihood of client change.

3. Helper and client come from similar social, cultural, racial, and economic backgrounds.

4. Helper and client are similar in their use of language, con- ceptual complexity, extroversion-introversion, objectivity- subjectivity, flexibility, and social awareness.

5. Helper and client are complementary or reciprocal in their need to offer and receive inclusion, control, and affection. The need for inclusion is related to associating, belonging, and companionship versus isolation, detachment, and alone- ness. Control is a power or influence dimension, and affec- tion refers to emotional closeness, friendliness, and the like. Helper and client are complementary or reciprocal on these dimensions if the level of inclusion, affection, or control that one member needs to offer approximates the level of that dimension that the other member needs to receive.

Obviously, no helper and client can be paired on all of these dimensions. However, it is probable that the greater the number of them reflected in a particular pairing, the more likely a favor- able relationship will develop.

Proxemics

Proxemics is the study of personal space and interpersonal distance. Is there a connection between how far apart two persons sit and their posture, on the one hand, and the favorability of their relationship, on the other hand? First, it does appear that liking in an interview setting leads to physical closeness and a particular type of posture. In an experiment by Leipold (1963), one group of college students was told, "We feel that your course grade is quite poor and that you have not tried your best. Please take a seat in the next room, and Mr. Leipold will be in shortly to discuss this with you." Other groups heard neutral or positive statements about their course performance. Those receiving praise subsequently sat significantly closer to the interviewer; those who were criticized chose to sit farther away.

A second study also suggests that increased liking leads to decreased physical distance. Walsh (1971) used distance and postural variations to investigate how attracted a group of patients was to an interviewer. Before each interview, an office was arranged so that the patient's chair was light, on wheels, and located at the other end of the room, 8 feet from where the interviewer sat. On entering the room, the interviewer suggested that the patient "pull up the chair." Attracted patients pulled the chair significantly closer to the interviewer than did unattracted patients.

The concern here, of course, is for relationship enhancement. Does close sitting and certain posturing *lead to* a favorable relationship, or are they the *result of* it? This question was tested in a modeling study (Goldstein, 1971). For some patients, the interviewer sat close by (27 inches) and assumed a posture shown in other research to reflect liking. Specifically, he leaned forward (20 degrees) toward the patient, maintained eye contact 90 percent of the time, and faced the patient directly (shoulder orientation of 0 degrees). Very different distance and posture were involved in the contrasting condition. The interviewer sat 81 inches from the patient, leaned backward 30 degrees, showed eye contact 10 percent of the time, and faced partially away from the patient, with a shoulder orientation of 30 degrees. Results of this research did in part show that distance and posture can indeed influence patient liking. As is true for helper-client matching, relevant research on proxemics is not abundant. However, proximity and an "interested" posture can be viewed as probable relationship enhancers.

What other suggestions or leads have been offered toward the goal of relationship enhancement? Heppner and Claiborn (1988) have reported that, on their index of relationship quality (namely, client willingness to see the therapist), positive scores were associated with therapist self-involving statements, a positive reputation, congruence between the therapist's verbal and nonverbal behaviors, and avoidance of the use of profanity. Strean (1985) urges that relationships are positive when the therapist is a "benign listener" who helps clients express negative feelings (including those toward the therapist) without censure when they appear. Safran, Muran, and Samstag (1994) draw much the same conclusion in their examination of "confrontation ruptures." Safran and Muran (2000) suggest the value of therapist tentativeness in offering observations, in acknowledging one's subjectivity, in accepting responsibility for one's contribution to the therapeutic interaction, and in recognizing that hope fades and may need to be rekindled. In addition, at times relationships in therapy grow more positive when client resistances are not only acknowledged but also legitimatized. Safran and Muran term this "allying with the resistance"—that is, reframing such avoidance as necessary, adaptive, and understandable. Lazarus (1993) raises the relationship-promoting notion of the therapist as an "authentic chameleon," one who offers differing interpersonal styles to different clients as the latter seem to prefer:

> Decisions are made on when and how to be directive, non-directive, supportive, cold, warm, reflective, gentle, tough, formal, informal, or humorous. Would the client prefer the therapist to take the stance of a coach or trainer rather than that of a warm empathic counselor? These issues are all considered important in forming a good therapeutic alliance with the client. (p. 163)

In the same responsive, prescriptive spirit, Lazarus also offers "bridging" and "tracking" as additional relationship-enhancing means in the context of his multimodal behavior therapy. Bridging occurs when the therapist keys into the client's preferred channel, style, or mode of processing and responding (e.g., affective, cognitive, other). Tracking involves analyzing the components constituting the client's problem or difficulty and the sequence in which these components emerge, then employing a sequence of intervention modalities matched to fit.

Cullari (1996) has proposed that therapist-client relationships evolve through stages and that differing enhancement efforts are required at different stages. During the first stage, Exploration, the relationship will take root in a positive manner if the therapist seeks to demystify the client's difficulties and make them seem more manageable. Self-efficacy heightening is a key goal of this opening period—the client is encouraged to believe that he or she has the abilities to resolve the presenting difficulties. Cullari calls his second relationship stage Identifying Personality Patterns and Tolerance. Optimal therapist behaviors here are being "consistent, concrete, predictable, logical, and reliable" (p. 144). The third stage, Commitment, is the phase in which a working alliance has been formed and the parties work cooperatively toward the goal of client change. Here, crucial for the relationship is continued agreement on the targeted problems, causes, and solutions. Finally, about the Growth or Stagnation stage, Cullari notes that,

> as clients struggle with making changes and experience the discomfort and difficulty most meaningful changes require, they are likely to become temporarily demoralized, dependent, angry, ambivalent, or hopeless. Consequently, the strength of the relationship also tends to plateau at this point. Therefore, at this stage it is important for the therapist to be very supportive and to listen actively to what clients have to say. (p. 145)

CONCLUSIONS

The degree of detail provided in this chapter on the existing technology of psychotherapeutic relationship enhancement is an accurate gauge of my belief that a positive therapist-client relationship lies at the core of efforts to manage and reduce client resistance. However, my overriding perspective on essentially all aspects of psychotherapy is prescriptive (Goldstein, 1978; Goldstein & Stein, 1976). Optimal conditions vary from client to client, a truism that also applies to relationship-enhancement efforts.

A ready example of this prescriptive perspective concerns empathy. Research of the past decade not only confirms exceptions to the finding that high levels of perceived therapist empathy are facilitative, it also suggests that such helper behaviors can have a negative influence on the therapeutic relationship in certain samples of clients. The following statements are of particular relevance to client resistance:

> While it is perhaps the most widely held (non-prescriptive) belief in contemporary psychotherapies of all types that an empathic and genuine therapist-patient relationship is a necessary and at times even sufficient facilitator of patient change (Patterson, 1966; Rogers, 1957; Truax & Carkhuff, 1967), the possibility that this generalization might not hold with at least some sub-types of juvenile delinquents has appeared sporadically in the delinquency literature for at least the last 25 years (Edelman & Goldstein, 1984; Goldstein, Heller, & Sechrest, 1966; Redl & Wineman, 1957; Schwitzgebel, 1961; Slack, 1960). Characteristic of this perspective is the early statement by Redl and Wineman (1957) specifically warning against overwhelming the delinquent with a close therapeutic relationship and recommending instead that a benevolent but somewhat impersonal and objective style of interaction might more likely lead to favorable therapeutic events, especially in the early stages of treatment. An identical perspective has been operationalized in such therapies as "experimenter-subject psychotherapy," Slack's (1960) "streetcorner research," (Schwitzgebel, 1961), Stollak and Guerney's (1964) "minimal contact therapy," Sechrest and Strowig's (1962) recommended use of teaching machines, and our own suggestions in this context regarding the likely prescriptive utility of impersonal, machine, and action therapies. (Goldstein et al., 1966)

It is not only delinquent youngsters for whom less, or at least different, might be better than more for relationship-enhancement purposes. DeVoge and Beck (1978) have described a broad range of clients for whom the closeness, friendliness, and empathy of a typical therapist-patient relationship could be highly aversive.

What then ought to be offered to such clients, beyond the aforementioned "impersonal and objective" approach? Stated otherwise, are prescriptively useful means currently available to enhance the quality of the therapeutic relationship for what might be termed "low relatability" clients? Although this matter has not received much empirical scrutiny, given the sheer numbers of such persons, it clearly should. Potentially effective relationship-enhancing techniques for use with such persons are already apparent. Specifically, these include the following:

1. Employing a less authoritarian structure, maintaining patient permission, and acceding to patient need for autonomy and even power (Beutler, 1982)

2. Providing a high degree of choice with minimal requirements for justification, seeking initial compliance under conditions of low external pressure, and using reattributional training to enhance self-attribution to responsibility (T. A. Willis, 1982)

3. Using interpretive modeling, antisabotage procedures, and paradoxical prescriptions (Rosenthal & Steffek, 1991)

4. Building on patient variability, acknowledging patient beliefs while challenging them, and selectively using overnurturance (Wachtel, 1980)

5. Employing other social-psychological (Higginbotham et al., 1989), paradoxical (Bogden, 1982), and eclectic (Lambert, 1982) procedures

To sum up very briefly, the need for relationship enhancement is considerable, the present technology includes many good leads, and the empirical work remains largely to be done.

CHAPTER 4

Compliance

The term *compliance* has appeared in the literature on client resistance with two quite different meanings. In research and clinical writings in behavioral medicine, compliance is defined as adherence to recommended or prescribed treatment regimens. Does the client comply/adhere to the prescribed course of medication or the recommended change in lifestyle? Its second meaning is *coercion,* in works dealing with the involuntarily mandated client, sentenced to treatment by legal, school, or other authorities. Does he or she show up for the initial session, speak up if so, and otherwise participate? The present chapter focuses on compliance in both of its usages—adherence and coercion—as a means for resistance reduction.

COMPLIANCE AS ADHERENCE

Compliance with treatment recommendations or prescriptions has been defined operationally in a number of ways. Some definitions are numerical, presented in terms of the percentage of recommended medications actually taken, number of life-change steps taken, and so forth. Not unlike definitions of client-initiated termination of psychotherapy as "dropout" or "attrition" after 2 or 6 or 12 sessions, numerical definitions are quite arbitrary and very much in the eye of the beholder. General definitions are helpful, though they lack the specificity of the (equally vulnerable) numerical definitions. Cullari (1996), for example, offers the following:

> Treatment adherence covers a broad range of behaviors including cooperating with the therapy process, taking prescribed medications, completing homework assignments, not engaging in self-destructive behaviors, and following treatment recommendations. (p. 66)

Given the benefits but also the real deficiencies of both numerical and general definitions of compliance as adherence, a more individualized or idiographic definition seems appropriate. Compliance can be understood only relative to the individual problem it seeks to alter. Gordis (1976) defined compliance as "the point below which the desired preventive or desired therapeutic result is unlikely to be achieved" (p. 52). While still general, such an individualized definition is considerably more functional than the foregoing and therefore is the view I will employ in this chapter.

Meichenbaum and Turk (1987) concretized their perspective on noncompliance by proposing that it consists of the behaviors listed in Table 4.1. The rates at which the behaviors indicated occur are apparently considerable.

Haynes, Taylor, and Sackett (1979) have reported that 20 to 30 percent of clients fail to follow relief-of-symptom medication regimens; 30 to 40 percent do not comply with preventive recommendations; and, when long-term medication is prescribed, 50 percent fail to adhere. DiMatteo and DiNicola (1982) found that 30 to 40 percent of clients fail to keep appointments for curative regimens, and 50 to 60 percent do not show up for preventive programming. According to Stimson (1974), 20 to 50 percent of clients fail to appear for their scheduled appointments. When they do appear, 20 to 60 percent of those prescribed medication will stop taking it prior to the time they have been instructed to do so, 19 to 74 percent will not follow instructions, 25 to 60 percent will make self-administration errors (with 35 percent of these errors threatening to the client's health). Blackwell (1992) indicates that each year in the United States approximately 240 million prescribed medications will not be taken at all, and a similar number will not be taken according to instructions. Jennings and Ball (1982), supplementing the dropout rates cited in chapter 1, report the same degree of nonadherence (50 percent) for psychotherapy referrals as that reported for patients who do not take prescribed medication. In comparison with Jennings and Ball's incidence level of 50 percent for "never shows," Baekeland and Lundwall (1975) noted an attrition rate after but one session of 20 to 57 percent for clients seen in mental health clinics. Pelham and Murphy (1986) reported similar rates of discontinuation for parents bringing their children for behavior modification interventions. Bringing

Table 4.1
Different Forms of Treatment Nonadherence

DRUG ERRORS

Failure to fill the prescription

Filling the prescription but failing to take the medication or taking only a portion of it

Not following the frequency or dose instructions of the prescription

Taking medication not prescribed

TREATMENT ATTENDANCE

Delay in seeking care

Failure to enter treatment programs

Not keeping appointments

Premature termination

BEHAVIORAL CHANGES

Not taking recommended preventive measures

Incomplete implementation of instructions

Sabotaging of treatment regimen

Nonparticipation in prescribed health programs

Creating one's own treatment regimens to "fill in the gaps" of what one believes one's health care provider is overlooking

Substituting one's own program for the recommended treatment regimens

Note. From *Facilitating Treatment Adherence* (p. 30) by D. Meichenbaum and D. C. Turk, 1987, New York: Plenum. Reprinted by permission.

medication and mental disorder data together, Blackwell (1979) and Ley (1979) both found that 25 to 50 percent of psychiatric outpatients, and more than half of schizophrenic or bipolar patients, do not take their medications as prescribed, or do not take them at all. Across all types of clients, Meichenbaum and Turk (1987) have reported

> the highest rates of adherence occurring for treatment
> with direct medication (injections, chemotherapy), high
> levels of supervision and monitoring, and acute onset . . .
> the lowest adherence rates with patients who have
> chronic disorders, when no immediate discomfort or
> risk is evident, when life-style changes are required,

and when prevention instead of palliation or cure is the desired outcome. (p. 24)

Blackwell (1997) summarizes much of the incidence data by noting that, across over 50 illnesses and conditions studied in the 12,000-plus articles dealing with compliance in the past 25 years, noncompliance in one form or another occurs in approximately 25 percent of inpatients and 50 percent of outpatients.

Sources and Correlates of Noncompliance

The following discussion concerns what the research literature has had to offer regarding sources and correlates of the types of noncompliance listed in Table 4.1, as well as regarding means for reducing such resistances. It is important to note at the outset that the view of resistance as both an intrapsychic phenomenon and function of therapist-client interaction, outlined in chapter 1, also applies in the context of behavioral medicine. Client resistance may reside in the client, in the client-therapist interaction, or both. Thus, the discussion of sources and correlates of noncompliance that follows explores client and relationship domains, qualities of the intervention itself, and the context in which the intervention is offered.

Client Characteristics

When examining qualities of the noncompliant individual, as well as in later discussion of interventions to improve compliance, the distinction between involuntary and voluntary noncompliance is important (Ley, 1979). *Voluntary noncompliance* takes place when clients agree to follow a recommended or prescribed treatment program but fail to do so due to forgetfulness, misunderstanding, time constraints, costs, or other circumstances. Interventions for this type of noncompliance might include altered economic arrangements, procedures to improve memory, clearer or simpler instructions, or other training. With involuntary noncompliance, the individual understands the treatment but either disagrees with it or, on other bases, chooses not to follow it. In this instance, intervention might include an educational or persuasive approach and perhaps actively encouraging "ownership" of the treatment effort by soliciting the client's participation in its choice and planning. As both Cullari (1996) and Ley (1979) recommend, it is important to identify the origins of client noncompliance before seeking to modify it.

Most important, the nature of the client's problem or disorder is associated with his or her likelihood of complying with the treatment protocol. Clients experiencing recognizable and unpleasant symptoms that are likely to be relieved via compliance are indeed more likely to comply. Adherence is lowest, note Meichenbaum and Turk (1987), when the treatment recommendations or instructions are prophylactic and to be carried out in the absence of distressing symptoms. Even when recognizable symptoms are present, some clients may adapt to them or view them as "normal" in their own case, and hence not see the need for or comply with recommended treatment. In general, Haynes (1976a) suggests, clients are more likely to comply when following treatment recommendations that require them to learn new behaviors (e.g., an exercise regimen) than when treatment focuses on changing old behaviors (e.g., reducing fat in one's diet). As Cullari (1996) notes, clients are least likely to comply when instructed to eliminate well-established habits (e.g., substance abuse, smoking), when they have chronic but not life-threatening conditions, and when the benefits of treatment are not immediately obvious.

The client's ability to process treatment-relevant information provided by his or her change agent is a well-investigated aspect of noncompliance. Dunbar and Agras (1980) found that two-thirds of patients forgot their diagnosis and treatment plan, and half could not recall instructional statements immediately after an office visit. Higbee, Dukes, and Bosso (1982) put a series of questions to clinic clients following a visit in which medication was prescribed. These questions concerned the name of the drug, its route of administration, frequency and timing, dosage, and duration of treatment. Clients were able to recall less than 50 percent of this information correctly. Similar information-processing failures as a basis for noncompliance have been reported by Boczkowski, Zeichner, and DeSanto (1985); Cassata (1978); and Mazzuca (1982). Cassata summarizes these results:

1. Patients forget much of what their doctors tell them.

2. Instructions and advice are more likely to be forgotten than other information.

3. The more a patient is told, the greater the proportion he or she will forget.

4. Patients will remember what they are told first.

5. Intelligent patients do not remember more than less intelligent patients.

6. Older patients remember as much as younger ones.

7. Moderately anxious patients remember more than highly anxious patients or patients who are not anxious.

Client beliefs about their presenting problem and its remediation significantly influence the likelihoood of compliance. Meichenbaum and Turk (1987) identify a number of beliefs likely to undermine compliance:

1. You take medicine only when you are ill and not when you feel better.

2. You need to give your body some rest from medicine once in a while, or otherwise your body becomes too dependent on it or immune to it.

3. The medicine is so powerful that it should only be used for brief periods of time.

4. When my child's symptoms go away I can stop using the medicine.

5. I resent being controlled by drugs.

6. God will take care of my illness.

7. Nothing I do seems to help.

More generally, client beliefs about how susceptible they are to a given disorder, how severe the disorder is, the likely benefits of the treatment program in resolving the disorder, and the costs or barriers to participating in it each substantially influence compliance (Horne & Weinman, 1998).

Diagnostically, Blackwell (1979), Cullari (1996), and Haynes (1979) report that noncompliance tends to be more likely in individuals who are drug or alcohol abusers; who have eating disorders, posttraumatic stress disorder, or disorders characterized by high levels of anxiety; or who suffer from disorders that impair cognitive processes, such as schizophrenia or psychotic depression.

Other client qualities that have been suggested as correlates of or influences upon noncompliance include client fear, guilt, fatalism, apathy, pessimism, shame, self-sufficiency, previous noncompliance, competing cultural concepts of disease and treatment, demandingness, need to avoid control by others, reactance, low expectation of intervention benefit, and dissatisfaction with treatment.

Treatment Characteristics

Noncompliance grows not only from the client. It is an interactive consequence of client, treatment, relationship, and extra-treatment forces. Stone (1979) found that nonadherence was 15 percent when one drug was prescribed, 25 percent when the client was asked to take two or three medications, and 35 percent if more than five drugs were prescribed. Malahey (1966) reports noncompliance to be greater the greater the number of times per day the medication is prescribed. The longer the client is required to wait before treatment begins, the more complex the treatment is, and the longer its duration, the greater the noncompliance (Sackett & Haynes, 1976). Treatments that require mere passive cooperation from the client and therapies administered by staff in hospital or clinic yield better compliance than those requiring active cooperation from the client. Compliance improves with continuity of care, as opposed to the not uncommon outpatient clinic arrangement of the client's being seen by the first available doctor. This is but one of several findings highlighting the central role in the compliance process of the client–change agent relationship. DiMatteo (1979); Foulkes, Persons, and Merkel (1986); and Haynes (1976b) are among the many investigators reporting a strong positive association between relationship quality and compliance. As Meichenbaum and Turk (1987) note, "Insofar as HCPs [health care providers] adopt an open, honest, supportive style, demonstrate respect, praise the patient, and provide clear expectations, treatment adherence will increase" (p. 63). Conversely, Becker and Rosenstock (1984) assert that

> patterns of communication which deviate from the normative doctor-patient relationship will be associated with patient's failure to comply with doctor's advice. Such deviations include circumstances where tension in the interaction is not released, and where the clinician

is formal, rejecting, controlling, disagrees completely with the patient, or interviews the patient at length without subsequent feedback. (p. 46)

Meichenbaum and Turk (1987) summarize in Table 4.2 the numerous ways demonstrated in the research literature that change agents may interfere with clear and effective communication with their clients. As Meichenbaum and Turk put it, many errors and oversights contribute to the "art of being a facilitator of nonadherence" (p. 78).

As is the case for the evidence reviewed in chapter 3 for psychotherapeutic intervention, in the context of behavioral medicine client–change agent relationship qualities are a major influence on client compliance.

Client–change agent relationships take place in an organizational context, and the context, too, enters the mix of compliance-influencing variables. Relevant here are such matters as who referred the client for treatment; the substance of that referral and its effect upon client expectancy and treatment-associated information; the waiting time between referral and intake; the quality and content of the intake process; the waiting time between intake and treatment initiation; the waiting time from arrival until the initial session begins; the continuity or discontinuity of care just noted; and much more about the setting, the treatment of the client by ancillary staff, and a host of other organizational features.

Interventions for Noncompliance

A substantial array of compliance-enhancing interventions have been described in the clinical and research literature concerning behavioral medicine. Most interventions fall into one of three categories: relationship enhancement, education, and behavior modification. Most clinicians wisely incorporate facets of all three of these categories. Chapter 3 focuses on the current technology of relationship enhancement as it has been implemented and evaluated in the context of psychotherapy. I see little if any reason why this technology—essentially as is—does not apply equally well toward the goal of compliance enhancement and resistance reduction in the context of behavioral medicine. The next two categories require more explanation.

Table 4.2
Change-Agent Contributions to Ineffective Communication

Act unfriendly, distant, demonstrate a lack of warmth, concern, interest. Be unapproachable and impersonal. Demonstrate disagreement, formality, and rejection. For example, fail to introduce yourself.

Look and act busy—watch clock, look out at waiting room to see how many more patients there are.

See patients in a chaotic setting where there are many interruptions (e.g., telephone calls, interruptions from nurse or secretary). Read case notes while interviewing patient.

Mumble, use medical jargon when speaking to the patient. Never ask if patient understands.

Ask patients specific close-ended questions requiring "yes" or "no" answers.

Cut off or interrupt patient statements.

Ignore patient's questions. Say you will come back to it, but don't.

Don't allow patients to tell their story in their own words.

Don't allow patients to express their ideas and concepts about their illness.

Fail to take into account patients' concerns and expectations.

Treat the disease instead of the patient ("What is the problem?" instead of "How are you?").

Omit clear-cut explanations of diagnosis and causes of illness.

Fail to state precise treatment regimen to be followed or state it in an unclear or too technical a fashion.

Ignore opportunities to give patient feedback.

Fail to solicit feedback from patient.

Adopt a hostile, suspicious, moralizing, low-empathy, and high-power-struggle stance. Fail to make eye contact or to sit at the same level as the patient. Keep a desk or some other physical obstacle between you and patient.

Abruptly terminate the interview.

Provide little support.

Note. From *Facilitating Treatment Adherence* (p. 78) by D. Meichenbaum and D. C. Turk, 1987, New York: Plenum. Reprinted by permission.

Education

The second and perhaps clinically most popular intervention category is education. Haynes, Wang, and DaMota-Gomes's (1987) analysis of evaluation research in this context reveals a success rate (increased compliance) of about 50 percent for educational interventions. The educational tactics that appear to facilitate compliance are participatory rather than persuasive. As Brody (1980) puts it, "Patients need to be seen as active participants in the clinical decision-making process, collaborators and allies who share responsibilities in the treatment regimen" (p. 80). Eisenthal, Emery, Lazare, and Udin (1979) and Schulman (1979) both report higher levels of compliance when the client has a significant role as co-developer in the intervention process. Beyond participation, the major target in educational intervention has been improving client (and change-agent) communication clarity and effectiveness, and reducing client forgetfulness.

According to Anderson and Kirk (1982), Coleman (1985), Hanson (1986), and Seltzer and Hoffman (1980), communication between client and change agent will be enhanced and compliance improved if the following steps are followed when prescribing a treatment regimen:

1. Select the information you give to clients carefully. The fewer the instructions, the more likely they are to be remembered and followed.

2. Tailor the directions to fit clients' vocabulary, educational level, socioeconomic background, and current functioning level.

3. Be clear, concrete, and specific (avoid generalities). Use short sentences and avoid scientific jargon.

4. It is better to give short bits of information at each meeting, if possible, as opposed to a lot of information all at once.

5. Give the most important instructions first.

6. Establish a trusting, supportive relationship, and demonstrate interest in clients.

7. Identify target and accessory symptoms before discussing medication effects.

8. Assess clients' expectations, beliefs about illness (cause, severity, course). Conduct an adherence-oriented history.

9. Describe to clients the condition, how it is to be treated, and the kind of medication or form of treatment required. Give a rationale and justification for the drug use and treatment strategy, and comment on goals of treatment. Include an understandable explanatory model of how and why medication should be effective.

10. Simplify the regimen if possible. Minimize different medications, number of doses, and schedule variations.

11. Prioritize treatment in a stepwise fashion, introducing components of the regimen in a gradual manner.

12. Give the name of the medications or treatments, and check to see that clients know these.

13. Describe the specific purpose and function of the prescribed medications or treatments. Tell the clients what the treatment does.

14. Repeat important points when possible.

15. Use concrete examples, modeling, analogies, acronyms, or videotapes.

16. Emphasize how important it is to follow the treatment directions.

17. If possible, allow clients to call you if they have questions or run into problems.

18. Check clients' comprehension. Question directly about medication. Ask the clients to repeat key points. Encourage them actively to reword the instructions. Ask them, Do you know what you are taking? When should you take it? How much do you need to take? What if you miss a dose?

19. Consider immediate and delayed beneficial consequences. Make sure clients understand that some medications take time to exert their effects. Stress that long-term benefits outweigh short-term inconvenience.

20. Encourage discussion concerning cost and risks versus benefits of following the treatment regimen.

21. Assess the clients' attitude toward medication prophylaxis, side effects, fears about being "controlled" by a drug, and concerns about addiction and social stigma.

22. Discuss and reduce fear of possible side effects and problems associated with medication or treatment.

23. Discuss ways in which clients can self-monitor. Help them devise ways to remember medication.

24. Caution about drug-drug, drug-food, and other therapeutic contraindications.

25. Give simple, typed information sheets that outline reasons for taking the drugs, the actions, dosage schedules, side effects, and what clients should do if side effects occur.

26. If appropriate, involve significant others (spouses, family members, community agencies) in the supervision of medication schedules.

27. Encourage clients to write down any questions or concerns as they come up and bring them in the next visit.

28. Ensure that clients feel they can follow the treatment regimen.

29. Ask about adherence at the next session.

30. Never assume that adherence is satisfactory. Make adherence a priority, specifically and routinely inquiring about it.

Table 4.3, drawn from the seminal work of Meichenbaum and Turk (1987), enumerates the educational and instructional techniques that have been employed to reduce noncompliance because of client forgetfulness.

Behavior Modification

A full array of behavior modification techniques have been employed in the context of behavioral medicine to increase adherence to program. Many have been quite successful (Barofsky, 1987; Epstein & Cluss, 1982; Epstein & Masek, 1978). Haynes et al.'s (1987) summary of relevant studies of this type indicates an 82-percent compliance success rate. Self-regulation techniques are high on this list. Because goal setting, self-monitoring, self-reinforcement, and the like are taught by the change agent but taken over and carried out by the client, detailed discussion of these techniques appears in chapter 5, on client empowerment as a strategy for resistance reduction. Beyond self-regulation methods, what other behavior modification means have been successfully employed to enhance compliance? They are numerous and diverse, including behavioral contracting (Dunbar & Agras, 1980; Steckel & Swain, 1977); corrective feedback (Epstein, Figueroa,

TABLE 4.3
Interventions to Reduce Patients' Forgetfulness

REMINDERS TO KEEP APPOINTMENTS

Mail reminders

Telephone cueing

Reminder cards with date and time of next appointment

Verbal and written commitments

Follow-up file for noting and contacting those who do not keep appointments

Decreased waiting times

Limited time interval between screening assessment and initial appointment and between telephone reminder and appointment

Individualized appointments for a specific health care provider at a particular time

Appointments at the most convenient time for the patient

REMINDERS TO TAKE MEDICATION

Wristwatches with alarms or small pocket timers

Drug reminder charts (e.g., time charts posted on bathroom wall)

Written memory aides (e.g., stickers on the refrigerator door or a sign posted on the medicine chest)

Tear-off calendars or pill calendars that are kept close to medication

Special medication dispensers such as homemade dose packs of a separate pill bottle for each day's needs or a special pill bottle to be carried in lunch box (Such dispensers provide feedback on dosages taken and missed.)

Special pill packages that have time alarm reminders or display pills to be taken by date

Strip packages that contain one day's dose of medication

Prescription stickers on medicine bottles that have the time circled

Stickers with directions for administration placed in a highly visible place in the home

Highly visible strategic location for placement of medication (e.g., pills taped to calendar)

Daily medication intake coordinated with the patient's specific routine (e.g., medication before brushing teeth or after breakfast)

Asking the patient to bring in bottle of pills on next visit or keep a record or diary of which pills are taken each day and at what times

Supervision—call patient, have patient call office once a week, involve family members

---

TABLE 4.3 (continued)

REMINDERS TO FOLLOW TREATMENT REGIMEN

Performance charts put in a prominent place (e.g., on bathroom wall)

Wristwatch with an alarm on it

Integration of the treatment adherence behavior into the patient's daily routine

Identification of reminders or cues for action

Rehearsal of treatment measures so they can be smoothly implemented

---

Note. From *Facilitating Treatment Adherence* (p. 140) by D. Meichenbaum and D. C. Turk, 1987, New York: Plenum. Reprinted by permission.

Farkas, & Beck, 1981); a variety of contingency management techniques (e.g., differential reinforcement, extinction, shaping; Barofsky, 1987; Brownell & Foreyt, 1985); modeling (of self-care procedures; Barofsky, 1987); desensitization (to aversions; Barofsky, 1987); problem-solving skills training (Davis & Glaros, 1986; Gilchrist, Schinke, Bobo, & Snow, 1986); interpersonal skills training (Ary, Toobert, Wilson, & Glasgow, 1986); and attributional retraining (to enhance self-efficacy; Meichenbaum & Turk, 1987).

Noncompliance, defined as nonadherence to recommended or prescribed regimens in behavioral medicine, is a widespread problem. The relationship-enhancing, educational, and behavior modification means for addressing this challenge and enhancing compliance are substantial and, as several clinicians and investigators have suggested, ought wisely to be employed together in potent intervention combinations.

Homework Assignments: A Compliance Case Study

Variously labeled home practice, extra-treatment practice, behavioral assignments, and between-therapy activity, homework assignments facilitate generalization of newly learned behaviors from the therapy setting to the client's real world of home, school, work, and other settings.* They keep the person

---

*For its relevance to compliance, I reprise discussion of homework from my book *Lasting Change: Methods for Enhancing Generalization of Gain* (Goldstein & Martens, 2000), where the topic appeared in the context of self-regulation.

"on task" while not in the clinic or consulting room. In addition to these central "feedforward" functions, homework successes and failures can feed back to the intervention itself, continually shaping its content and process in productive ways. Finally, homework assignments in the context of psychotherapy permit intervention access to an array of behaviors that cannot easily be observed, simulated, or treated in the therapist's office because they are too private (e.g., sexual), infrequent (e.g., tantrums), frequent (e.g., eating), or broadly defined (e.g., marital conflict). More generally, the positive consequences of homework assignments for the acquisition and/or maintenance of behavior have been amply demonstrated in a number of investigations (Fennell & Teasdale, 1987; Kazdin & Mascitelli, 1982; Maultsby, 1971; Neimeyer & Feixas, 1990; Persons, Burns, & Perloff, 1988; Prochaska, Wilcox, & Rossi, 1988; Shelton, 1973; Zettle & Hayes, 1987).

Dunlap (1932), Herzberg (1947), Karpman (1949), and Salter (1949) were early proponents of task assignment. Kelly's (1955) fixed-role therapy was a major advance in elaborating and refining such usage. Here, clients, with intervenor assistance, constructed a positive persona for functioning in the real world in a less problematic manner (the fixed-role sketch) and were then assigned the task of living out that role in the natural environment. Masters and Johnson (1970) systematized the use of task assignments in their employment of this technique in the context of sex therapy.

Instigation Therapy Procedures

The utilization of homework assignments in psychotherapy begins, where perhaps all therapeutic procedures should begin, with a careful and thorough explanation to the client of the procedure and its purposes. This structuring not only provides a motivation-enhancing rationale but also provides a forum for the client's anticipation and resolution of likely problems of commitment and compliance.

Once the client is familiar with and accepting of the homework strategy, specific assignments may be planned and carried out. Planning, or goal setting, typically is primarily conducted by the therapist early in treatment (though even here, only with full goal acceptance by the client), with a major effort being made to involve the client increasingly in such goal setting as treatment progresses. In the later stages of the intervention, it is the client, not the therapist, who assumes primary goal-setting responsibility. Self-attributed change has been shown in a number of contexts to be maintained to a greater extent than change that is externally imposed—hence the importance of this gradual shift to client-determined goal setting.

Once the general goal of the homework assignment has been established, its parameters must be specified. Shelton and Levy (1981) have suggested the following elements be included:

1. A *do* statement, clearly indicating the specific behaviors to be carried out (e.g., "Read, practice, observe, count, say [a particular behavior].")

2. A *quantity* statement, defining how long or how often the behavior needs to be done (e.g., "Give four compliments per day"; "Write a list of 10 _____ .")

3. A *record* statement, specifying what is to be recorded and when (e.g., "Whenever that thought occurs, write _____ on the _____"; "Each time he hits, mark a _____ on the chart.")

4. A *bring* statement, indicating what the client is to bring to the next session (e.g., "Bring your spouse; your chart; your list.")

5. A *contingency* statement, spelling out what consequences are to follow each successful or unsuccessful task attempt (e.g., "Call for your next appointment after you have done _____"; "Each time you _____ , a dollar will be returned from your deposit.")

It is highly desirable that the homework assignment be put in writing, signed by the client, and copies retained by both intervenor and client. Doing so not only aids later evaluation of the attempt to execute the homework, it also increases the likelihood that the homework will be attempted in the first place.

The homework task having been set, the first step in its implementation is rehearsal or anticipatory practice in the safe confines of the treatment setting. At this juncture, the intervenor may serve as a structurer, model, clarifier, elaborator, and/or provider of rehearsal feedback.

Following the goal setting, task specification, and rehearsal procedures, the client carries out the assignment when, where, and with whom in the natural environment specified. What follows is a careful and detailed review by therapist and client of what actually transpired when the assignment was executed. The homework may have proceeded as planned. When this is the case, it is crucial that the intervenor generously praise the effort, highlight its achievement, and use the success as the basis for future assignments. If the effort failed in one or more of its aspects, the intervenor can praise the effort, if not the outcome, and use the information provided to regroup, reflect, and restructure a new (perhaps less ambitious) homework assignment. Rather than attempt to execute the assigned homework, and either succeeding or failing, the client may elect not to comply with the assignment. The following section concerns the sources of possible noncompliance and means for its remediation.

Noncompliance: Sources and Solutions

The reasons an individual may fail to complete, or even undertake, a given homework assignment are numerous and varied. Lazarus (1981) has catalogued some possibilities: The client sees the assignment as irrelevant to his or her current or future goals, too threatening to attempt, or too time consuming; there is insufficient clarity as to who is responsible for change; significant others sabotage or at least do not support the effort; and secondary gain maintains rather than moderates the problem behavior. Shelton and Levy (1981) have listed lack of assignment-relevant skills or knowledge and the pull of other competing or interfering behavior or cognitions. Primakoff, Epstein, and Covi (1986) have spoken of "compliance decay," referring to a pattern of creeping noncompliance in which early to midtreatment adherence to assignments decays with time, repetition, routine, or other influences. Some further influences on homework assignment noncompliance certainly concern intervenor characteristics or qualities of the therapist-client pair.

To a large extent, the sources for homework noncompliance suggest the means for moderating or ameliorating the problem. Irrelevant to goals—restructure goals or restructure assignments. Too threatening to attempt or too time consuming—have the client bite off a smaller piece or present the original assignment again in a different way. Insufficient clarity—clarify further and better. Generalized resistance—turn to the means described throughout this book to identify, explore, and moderate client resistance. Sabotage from significant others or high levels of secondary gain—accelerate the frequency and intensity of positive contingencies for homework completion.

In this same spirit of "letting the diagnosis suggest the cure," Shelton and Levy (1981) have recommended, first, that noncompliance due to inadequate client skills be met with enhanced instructions, additional skills training, graduating more slowly or finely the size and difficulty of assignments, and adding rehearsal attempts. Their recommendations for dealing with interfering cognitions are having the client make public and private commitments to comply (e.g., via contracting), seeking ways to identify and reduce the negative effects of compliance as perceived by the client, and using paradoxical strategies (e.g., insisting on noncompliance). Finally, their proposals for reducing environmental pull or rewards for noncompliance include, as noted, richer schedules of reinforcement for compliance and closer monitoring of real-world compliance from multiple sources.

Other suggestions to encourage homework compliance have been offered. J. S. Beck (1996) has recommended that clients be aided in distancing themselves from the assignment by presenting it as an experiment or a practice exercise—in much the same spirit as Kelly's (1955) fixed-role enactments. Shelton (1979) has urged that the client be given homework "veto power" over any particular assignment and that the earliest assignments be framed so that successful completion is particularly likely. Shelton also suggests frequent between-session phone calls from therapist to client to offer support and reminders along the homework route. Finally, and perhaps especially valuable, Beck et al. (1979) have encouraged change agents to anticipate noncompliance when the assignment is initially developed by having "clients imagine that they are undertaking the assignment while they are still in the therapist's office. This exercise sometimes helps them identify problems which can then be discussed before they leave the office" (p. xxx).

COMPLIANCE AS COERCION

In behavioral medicine the noncompliant individual fails to adhere to the proposed or prescribed program out of forgetfulness or reluctance or misunderstanding or a discrepant belief structure, as well as in response to aspects of the treatment, qualities of the change agent, or aspects of the client–change agent relationship. In compliance as coercion, the client elects non-compliance as part of a pattern of marked resistance. He or she is the involuntary, mandated client who has been "sentenced" to treatment by legal or school authorities or who has been "dragged" there by a threatening spouse, an insistent parent, or a won't-take-no-for-an-answer employer. Willis (1984) comments:

> Many clients sit in the therapist's office because they
> must. Civil courts often demand treatment; harassed and
> frantic parents often drag unwilling youngsters with
> them into family therapy; in the face of a diverse ultima-
> tum, a reluctant spouse often follows an aggrieved mate
> into marital therapy. Sometimes no option to attendance
> in therapy exists; sometimes therapy simply constitutes a
> reprieve from something worse. In either situation,
> attendance is compulsory, feels coercive, and is per-
> ceived as a violation of one's personal integrity. Who,
> indeed, wouldn't be reluctant in such a situation! (p. 40)

In addition to the mandated, the insistently prodded, and those under ultimatums, there are other categories of clients who are highly resistive, difficult to deal with, and come to therapy ambivalent at best. Wong's (1983) survey of senior clinicians described such clients as rejecting help, failing to cooperate, refusing medication, sabotaging treatment, and, at times, acting dangerously. Kottler (1992) stressed these clients' demandingness, need for control, and heavy reliance on externalization and projection of all their woes. A similar therapist survey by Robbins, Beck, Mueller, and Mizener (1988) led to a listing of most difficult clients as those who (a) refuse to cooperate, (b) appear unable to benefit from treatment, (c) demand extra time and attention, (d) have apparent potential to be violent, and (e) present a perplexing set of problems. Cullari (1996) pointed in this context to the terminating client who, from the opening session through the course of treatment, constantly threatens to quit. He or she frequently questions the therapist's competence, demands changes in scheduling or financial arrangements, and in other ways—without letup—communicates how much he or she does not want to be there. Diagnostically, it is frequently the case that the involuntary or highly resistive client is labeled paranoid, borderline, narcissistic, antisocial, or substance abusing (Kottler, 1992; Robbins et al., 1988).

Such clients are at one end of the continuum of client resistance. They present an array of treatment difficulties for the therapist and, more generally, are clients who—regardless of diagnosis—have their fannies in the chair but their eyes on the door. For all these clients, compliance with the treatment program is problematic at best, noxious at worst, and likely to be perceived by them as coercive.

Intervention Recommendations

Successful treatment of clients feeling coerced into treatment is challenging. Willis (1984) champions direct confrontation of the resistive behaviors such clients may display. Harris and Watkins (1987) urge patience and remind challenged clinicians that very little evidence suggests that confrontation is useful or appropriate in this context. In their view, the therapist's task is to be "supremely empathic." Cullari (1996) also recommends "go slowly," noting that such clients often require a lengthy (re-)orientation period. At times, a coerced client may be "hooked" into treatment by, Larke (1985) suggests, "return of his or her driver's license, completion of probation, or a positive report to family court" (p. 263).

Harris and Watkins (1987) suggest the following intervention sequence:

1. Give heavy doses of early empathy for relationship-establishing purposes. In particular, offer empathy with the feelings associated with coercion, such as anger, fear, and loss of control.

2. Provide structure and set/negotiate expectations. Contracting may prove useful here, especially with regard to treatment goals. Establish early a sense of shared power and reciprocity in decision making.

3. Provide as much choice as possible, and minimize demands. A simple example: Offer a selection of possible meeting times from which the client can choose, and set the meeting schedule a week at a time.

4. Help the client save face by recognizing, acknowledging, empathizing with, and seeking to defuse his or her embarrassment, fear of dependency, and similar affects associated with being mandated for treatment.

5. Show interest in the client, and express a sincere desire to help.

6. Try to find a problem, however small, that the client can agree to work on.

7. Bring into the open, question, and (gently) challenge the client's reluctance to participate.

8. Make clear to the client what you, the therapist, are and are not willing to tolerate. Agency rules and regulations need to be made explicit and followed.

Cullari (1996) reminds us to assure the client of confidentiality and notes that moderate self-disclosure by the therapist may build rapport and trust, as well as serve as a model to the client to respond in kind. Much like those of Cullari (1996) and Harris and Watkins (1987), the American Psychiatric Association's (1994) recommendations emphasize the earliest stages of treatment:

> Therapists must make every effort to elicit from the patient and then define and negotiate shared goals around which a treatment alliance can be established, regardless of how the patient first comes to treatment and regardless of what external motivating or coercing factors are operative. (p. 6)

> Formation of an alliance is fostered by therapists explicitly defining their role as agent of the patient, in contrast to working for the patient's parents, the hospital, or another institution that might be perceived by the patient as being in conflict with his or her own needs. (p. 7)

As can be seen, much of the intervention literature vis-à-vis coerced clients is client centered (i.e., go slow, be patient, offer large doses of empathy, avoid confrontation, negotiate goals, share power, etc.). In earlier discussion of relationship enhancement, evidence was presented that, at least for some categories of involuntary clients (i.e., delinquent youth), low levels of therapist empathy appear to be optimal (Edelman & Goldstein, 1984). This finding serves as another caution against too swiftly concluding that "one size fits all" when it comes to the treatment of clients feeling coerced into therapy.

Obviously, working with involuntary clients presents special challenges and often burdens for the therapist. As the American Psychiatric Association (1994) report notes:

> Outpatient commitment often fails when the clinic staff seems reluctant to be part of the process. Staff members may oppose coercive approaches, may dislike participating in forcing "clients" to come into treatment, and may even take the position that "forced treatment doesn't work." Staff members may also resent the extra paperwork that is often required with these patients, or they may be reluctant to have anything to do with the courts. (p. 70)

Yet coerced treatment does quite regularly work. Involuntary clients often do improve. If responsive to the outcome evidence, therapists need not be overly pessimistic and, in fact, as often as not can be hopeful of positive outcomes. Working with involuntary clients is arduous, however. Helpful recommendations are that therapists educate and coordinate their plans with their referral sources (Storch & Lane, 1989), that they make special efforts to understand and manage their countertransference reactions to such clients (Storch & Lane, 1989), that they avoid the possibility that viewing a client as "difficult" will function as a self-fulfilling prophecy (Cullari, 1996), and that they seek needed supervision of their work (Cullari, 1996).

As noted, involuntary clients often fare well. Laundergan, Spicer, and Kammerer (1979) report no difference in success rate between mandated or voluntary clients seeking to modify their use of alcohol. Ward and Allivise (1979) have speculated that a "motivational myth" may be operating here (i.e., the belief that voluntary clients are more open to treatment at its outset but then tend to drop out when symptoms are reduced). Mandated clients, in contrast, are coerced into persisting, remain in therapy even under duress, and eventually derive benefit. Other investigations comparing treatment outcomes for involuntary versus voluntary clients for the most part report no differences (Larke, 1985; Storch & Lane, 1989). Shah (cited in American Psychiatric

Association, 1994) is quite likely correct in his assertion that, "although many believe that treatment must be free of coercion to work, I think that is nonsensical. Medication, for example, works though coerced. I think psychotherapy is probably analogous" (p. 23).

SOCIAL SUPPORT

Whether speaking of adherence or coercion, of the forgetful client of behavioral medicine or the resentful client of mandated psychotherapy, compliance with treatment is substantially influenced by actions taken and not taken by significant others in the client's social network. The amount and nature of social support for compliant or noncompliant behavior and attitudes is particularly important. The behaviors of important others directed toward the client can function for better (i.e., increase compliance) or for worse (i.e., increase noncompliance). With regard to the positive function of social support, Meichenbaum and Turk (1987) note:

> The significant others can collaborate in identifying and implementing ways in which the patient could be helped in adhering to the treatment regimen (e.g., encourage, remind, assist, supervise, and reinforce patient for engaging in self-care behavior). Significant others can also identify possible obstacles and high-risk situations that might interfere with patient adherence. . . . In various programs, social support agents have participated in monitoring patient behavior, participating in commitment and behavior contracts, and engaging in joint activities. (p. 217)

Yet the behavior of significant others can be for worse and can increase noncompliance. Baranowski and Nader (1985) observe that

> there may be no aspects of family life that maximize compliance, but many aspects that inhibit and detract from compliance. These factors include lack of family cohesion, interference of the treatment regimen with social role tasks, secondary gains, scapegoating, family expectations, and the like. (p. 69)

Cullari (1996) similarly notes that social networks may function to enhance noncompliance. In the case of clients being treated for alcohol or drug abuse, for example, clients may have family members or friends with the very same problem who serve as encouragers or models of noncompliance. Families, he observes, may feel threatened by the treatment plan and its hoped-for consequences for the client, or it may be perceived as intrusive or in opposition to the customary ways a given culture deals with the problem. Any of these factors may yield social nonsupport or active interference with treatment and implementation plans.

The potential role of social support in the compliance effort is clearly quite significant, so much so that "it is likely not an overstatement to assert that figures in one's social network may at times hold in their hands the very destiny of who we are, what we do, and who we become" (Goldstein & Martens, 2000). Given the potency and relevance of social support to the resistance reduction process, subsequent discussion focuses on identifing both theoretically and operationally what social support is and on describing its specific impact on compliance behavior.

Early on, social support was defined by Caplan (1974) as the provision, in time of need, of information, cognitive guidance, tangible resources, and emotional sustenance. Cobb (1976) defined it more generally as "information leading the subject to believe that he/she is cared for and loved, esteemed and valued, that he/she belongs to a network of communication and mutual obligation" (p. 300). House (1981) saw social support as "an interpersonal transaction involving one or more of the following: (1) emotional concern (liking, love, empathy), (2) instrumental assistance (goods and services), (3) information (about the environment), or (4) appraisal (information relevant to self-evaluation)" (p. 3).

According to Albrecht and Adelman (1987), "Social support refers to verbal and nonverbal communication between recipients and providers that reduces uncertainty about the situation, the self, the other, or the relationship, and functions to enhance a perception of personal control in one's life experience" (p. 19). According to Jacobson (1986), social support is defined in terms of resources that meet needs. Emotional support refers to behavior that fosters feelings of comfort and leads an individual to believe that he or she is admired, respected, and loved, and that others are available to provide caring and security. Cognitive support refers to information, knowledge, and/or advice that helps the individual understand his or her world and adjust to changes within it. Material support refers to goods and services that help solve practical problems.

In addition to the view of social support as an instrumental, emotional, or stress-buffering resource, Fisher (1996) has suggested that it might be viewed simply as a commodity or reinforcer of behavior. From this perspective, and in a manner directly relevant to compliance enhancement, interactions with supportive social networks become incentives for choosing certain behaviors (e.g., health maintenance) over others (e.g., smoking or drug abuse). According to Fisher:

> Viewing social support as simply a good thing changes the view of its links to life expectancy, decreased health risks, emotional well-being, or stress management. Its benefits may be based on providing incentives for life-enhancing behavior as well as offsetting the impacts of stressors or events that might otherwise lead to emotional upset. For instance, it may be that the presence of social contact and support militates against depression directly by offsetting depressed mood in the same way that other, positively valued events offset depression. . . . So too, "having more to live for" in satisfying social relationships may provide incentives for quitting smoking, managing diabetes, learning the skills necessary to feel competent to care for a child, and the diverse other good things to which social support has been linked. (1996, p. 211)

Shumaker and Brownell (1984); Lin (1986); and Heller, Swindle, and Dusenbury (1986) each placed special emphasis in their definitions on social support as *perceived*, especially by its recipient. Thus, social support is "an exchange of resources between at least two individuals perceived by the provider or the recipient to be intended to enhance the well-being of the recipient" (Shumaker & Brownell, 1984, p. 17). Again, "a social activity is said to involve social support if it is perceived by the recipient of that activity as esteem enhancing or if it involves the provision of stress-related interpersonal aid (emotional support, cognitive restructuring, or instrumental aid)" (Heller et al., 1986, p. 467).

Barrera (1986) has suggested that the core ingredients across these diverse definitions are (a) social embeddedness, or a sense of connectedness; (b) the perception of support or assistance; and (c) the actual delivery of such support or assistance. Kahn and Antonucci (1980) saw the key elements of social support as affect (expressing liking, admiration, respect), affirmation (expressing agreement or acknowledgment), and aid (giving such assistance as information, labor, time, or money). Vaux (1988) sought to resolve the definitional discrepancy by asserting that social support is best viewed as a higher order metaconstruct comprising a number of legitimate and distinguishable subconstructs (definitions). According to Vaux, these subconstructs, or core definitional streams, include support network resources, supportive behavior, and subjective appraisals of support.

Some aspects of the definition of social support seem clear and are generally agreed on: its informational function, its affective implications, its perceptual basis, and its assistance content. Perhaps this examination of contemporary definitions of social support can best be summarized in the following final perspective, one that conveys especially well the essence of this elusive construct:

> *You are the wind beneath my wings.*
> *—Henley and Silbar*

> The line above . . . captures in a subtle but powerful
> image the role that social support plays in our lives. Our
> family and close friends, mentors and workmates,
> acquaintances and neighbors are always there—a social
> medium through which we pass. Like the wind, their
> presence is so ordinary as often to go unnoticed. Yet
> like the wind beneath a bird's wing, they are an essen-
> tial part of our flight—holding us up, carrying us along,
> providing life, allowing us to soar and to glide, giving
> us location and identity. . . . Social support has to do
> with everyday things—sharing tasks and feelings,
> exchanging information and affection. (Vaux, 1988, p. 1)

Expressions of Social Support

An understanding of what social support is and of the manner in which it functions will be enhanced by a survey of its various expressions or concretizations. People may enact social support by listening, expressing concern, showing affection, sharing a task, caretaking, lending money, giving advice, making suggestions, and socializing (Vaux, 1988). They may provide behavioral assistance, feedback, guidance, information, comfort, intimacy, services, or lay referrals (Shumaker & Brownell, 1984). Social support is expressed through concern, assistance, value similarity, positive interaction, and trust (Brim, 1974); emotional support, cognitive guidance, tangible assistance, and social reinforcement (Hirsch, 1980); help in mobilizing resources, managing emotional problems, sharing tasks, and providing material and cognitive assistance (Caplan, 1974); and provision of attachment, social integration, reassurance of worth, reliable alliance, guidance, and opportunity for nurturance (Weiss, 1974). Social support may be, as Berndt (1989) has suggested, esteem (or emotional) support, informational support, instrumental support, or companionship support. Its avenues of expression are many and varied indeed.

Consequences of Social Support

Social support provision has been held to protect individuals from the negative effects of stressful circumstances (the stress-buffer model) or to act directly to enhance a sense of well-being, independent of stressful circumstances and experiences (the direct-effect model). It can offer, according to Nietzel, Guthrie, and Susman (1990), (a) protective direct action, (b) inoculation, (c) appraisal guidance, (d) diversion, (e) problem-solving assistance, and (f) palliative emotional support. Social support has been held to promote satisfaction; a feeling of being cared for, respected, or involved; and a sense of attachment, belonging, or reliable alliance (Vaux, 1988). Sandler, Miller, Short, and Wolchik (1989) have suggested that it may protect self-esteem by both preventing the occurrence of esteem-threatening events and moderating the negative effects of stressful events on self-esteem. Social support may contribute substantially to illness prevention, recovery from diverse disorders, and stress reduction (Kuo & Tsai, 1986; Parry, 1986). It can promote feelings of personal control (Krause & Keith, 1989); reduce one's level of depression (Flaherty & Richman, 1989); and, as suggested by the now 5,000-plus studies of its sources and outcomes, quite possibly do a great deal more.

Other consequences of social support may be less beneficial and perhaps even harmful. Dependency on others may be promoted, and self-reliance and tolerance for dealing with discomfort may be diminished (Brownell & Shumaker, 1985). In addition, the support provided may be targeted to encourage inappropriate, abusive, or antisocial behaviors (Ferguson & Horwood, 1996).

Social Support Intervention

In most circumstances, for most presenting problems, for most clients, social support enhances compliance. This outcome has been demonstrated in treatment adherence studies of weight reduction, smoking, exercise, dental visits, alcoholism, dietary habits, taking medication, wearing orthopedic appliances, and others (Baekeland & Lundwall, 1975; Baranowski & Nader, 1985; Becker & Green, 1975; Brownell, Heckerman, Westlake, Hayes, & Monti, 1978; Colletti & Brownell, 1982; DiMatteo & DiNicola, 1982; Dunbar & Agras, 1980; Gonder-Frederick, Cox, Pohl, & Carter, 1984; Janis, 1983; Jay, Litt, & Durant, 1984). In all, as Haynes, Taylor, and Sackett's (1979) review of relevant studies concludes, about three-quarters of such research yields positive outcomes.

Social support intervention programming has typically distinguished between natural and constructed support. *Natural support* occurs and develops without the efforts of professionals, agencies, or other formal change agents. It is the emotional, informational, or material assistance provided by figures in one's own social network—family, friends, neighbors, and others—with no shaping, urging, or prompting by non-network others. *Constructed support,* also variously termed "contrived" (Vaux, 1988) and "grafted" (Gottlieb, 1988), involves similar forms of assistance that are, in a sense, artificially provided by formal and semiformal change agents. To the degree that social support provision yields benefits, it is more frequently the case that natural and not constructed support is responsible. Bryant (1985) has pointed out that the considerable amount of social support research on type of support, timing of support, and consequences of support has "lost sight of the crucial fact that it was the very existence of a prior relationship [between supporter and recipient] that brought supportive meaning to the interactions"

(p. 54). Aid efforts designed to provide support gained their supportive influence, Bryant believes, from the supporter-recipient relationship. Others hold a similar view. Vaux (1988) has noted that (in contrast to support provided by professionals) family, friends, and other natural helpers are readily accessible, understand the individual's world, already have an ongoing relationship with the individual, and can provide culturally sensitive and nonstigmatizing help. Hobfoll, Nadler, and Leiberman (1986) have asserted that closeness to the support provider is a major determinant of both the recipient's satisfaction with the support provided and the stress-buffering effectiveness of the support. Rook and Dooley (1985) added to this speculation by pointing out the difficulty in identifying and then extracting the active support ingredients in natural systems to then undertake the even more difficult task of constituting and implementing such ingredients to good effect in "unnatural" support systems.

The case for the superiority of natural support ought not be overstated, however. Heller and Rook (1997) have noted that stressors that impact a given individual may ripple through that individual's social network. Further, fellow network members may lack experience with the particular type of problem for which aid is needed, possess misguided or erroneous beliefs regarding optimal support processes and content, and become so overinvolved in the problem in question that their supportive efforts are inadequate or even counterproductive.

It is important to introduce the concept of the "uniformity myth" into this consideration of alternative sources of support. First suggested by Kiesler (1966) in the context of psychotherapy, the uniformity myth is the belief that what constitutes effective treatment is effective across all clients, therapists, and situations. In the context of social support and support source, it is important, as Heller, Price, and Hogg (1990) have noted, to avoid the uniformity myth and instead acknowledge the diversity of providers, recipients, and support. Vaux (1988) believes, and I agree, that when fuller evaluation data are available, "natural and professional helping may each be effective within their spheres, perhaps even performing complementary functions" (p. 261). Until such clarifying data are in fact available, and as a significant part of such an effort, a parsimonious intervention strategy would suggest a search to simultaneously seek to better understand and improve the effectiveness of *both* natural and constructed social support provision.

CONCLUSIONS

This chapter has examined the theme of resistance reduction in terms of compliance to treatment as offered. Both compliance as adherence and as coercion have been considered as discussion focused on behavioral medicine and treatment for involuntary clients, respectively. Sources of compliant and noncompliant behavior and resistance-reducing interventions have been the main topic, with special attention given to treater, relationship, treatment, and extra-treatment domains. With regard to this last domain, discussion centered on the nature and level of social support the client is likely to receive for compliant behavior. Much of this chapter concerns actions taken by others—for example, the change agent and members of the client's social network—as they influence client compliance. The chapter that follows focuses on client empowerment, describing a preferred approach to resistance reduction: providing the client with the power, control, and ability to select and manage his or her own treatment regimen, thus obviating a great deal of resistance in the first place.

CHAPTER 5

Client Empowerment

Client empowerment in the sense of setting one's own life goals, controlling the inner resources needed to reach those goals, and, more generally, living a life in which one has a major influence on one's daily experience and ultimate destiny is the goal of all psychotherapies. Autonomy, purposefulness, self-direction, independence, and choicefulness are aspects of empowerment. Yet in the vast majority of approaches such end-of-treatment client empowerment can only be attained through a therapy in which the client submits to an extended period of disempowerment. His or her behavior must be diagnosed, assessed, interpreted, modified, treated, or in other ways acted upon by the empowered external agent, the therapist. It is a paradox of most treatment approaches that planned and intensive disempowerment is the route to later empowerment. A major theme of this book is the recognition that a number of clients resist the disempowerment process; the therapy thus falters; and the autonomous, fully functioning outcome is never reached. Some clinicians have responded to this state of affairs by urging that client empowerment become not only the hoped-for end-of-treatment goal but also a core quality of the treatment process.

Empowerment as an orienting philosophy and set of operating procedures for resistance reduction grows from a long series of psychotherapeutic approaches. It is interesting that the philosophical ancestry of empowerment is quite diverse: nondirective (Rogers, 1957), strategic (Erickson, 1980), psychodynamic (Weiss & Sampson, 1986), experiential (Gendlin, 1981), and solution focused (DeShazer, 1985; O'Hanlin & Weiner-Davis, 1989). However, in its core strategies and tactics each approach to therapy is truly collaborative, yielding power, direction, and control of much of the process to the client. Though over the course of my own career I have read and become familiar with these approaches and their client empowerment qualities, my introduction to the clinical necessity for resistance reduction and the value of client empowerment came in my own applied work with delinquent youths.

NEGOTIATING THE CURRICULUM

In the early 1980s, my colleagues and I developed a social skills training curriculum we called Skillstreaming (Goldstein, Sprafkin, Gershaw, & Klein, 1980), which, in many of its applications, targeted aggressive and delinquent youth. When results of evaluations of Skillstreaming's efficacy found transfer and maintenance of gain to occur less often than we had hoped, we folded Skillstreaming into a more complex, multimodal intervention, Aggression Replacement Training (ART; Goldstein & Glick, 1987). This intervention consisted of Skillstreaming (its behavioral component), anger control training (its cognitive component), and moral reasoning training (its values component). Our first two evaluations of the effectiveness of ART (Goldstein & Glick, 1987) were conducted in residential delinquency facilities, one of medium security, the other, maximum. Resident participation in ART, like all else in these institutions, occurred on an involuntary basis. Much as youths were told to go to English class during the school part of the day or to their rooms or to a counseling session, they were told where and when to go for ART. The skills chosen for the Skillstreaming part of the ART curriculum were chosen by staff, not youths, with staff choices being made based on a survey inquiring into which 10 skills from the 50-skill curriculum each staff member felt the youths needed most. The outcomes of these two efficacy investigations were quite promising. A substantial number of the skills were learned well and aggressive behavior dropped substantially when compared with that of a control group. Moreover, there appeared to be some carryover of these desirable outcomes to the youths' functioning in the community for those released from custody in the year following our evaluations.

Given the encouraging findings in the faculty and community, we decided to undertake a much-needed, if more challenging, evaluation of ART for no longer incarcerated youths living in the community (Goldstein, Glick, Irwin, Pask-McCartney, & Rubama, 1989). To motivate the youths who were to participate in the community-based ART sessions—and, we hoped, to minimize their resistance to such participation—each youth was informed while he was still incarcerated that regular and reliable attendance at ART sessions was a firm condition of release. In addition, during the last 3 weeks of their incarceration, the youths were taken from the facility, brought to the city in which ART sessions were being held, observed/participated in a session, were allowed to stay overnight in their own homes, and the next day were returned to the facility. We speculated that the stick of the "must attend" condition of release and the carrot of the three extra home visits would set our effort to minimize participation resistance on a good course.

Yet as the targeted youths were released, with bus tokens and directions to the Division for Youth office in hand, it became clear that attendance at ART sessions was not what we had hoped. To make the trip easier, we hired a van and driver to go to the youths' homes just before each scheduled session and pick them up. Far too often, the driver would knock on the front door, and the youth would leave his house by the back door. Resistance in the form of nonattendance was far from reduced. We decided to take a different tack.

Rather than continuing to teach the Skillstreaming skills of *our* choice in these sessions, or those selected by facility staff in the survey noted earlier, we decided to consult the participating youths themselves. Though such youngsters tend to externalize their life difficulties ("Ain't nothing *my* fault!") and minimize any difficulties they do acknowledge, it is nonetheless true that after a year or more of incarceration, return to community living is often accompanied by a host of family, peer, school, work, and other adjustments, readjustments, and problems. First through individual and, when possible, small-group discussions with youths, we actively sought to identify and explore these daily living challenges. Our goal was not counseling or verbal remediation. Instead, our purpose was for them to collaborate with us to select the most relevant skills. These were indeed empowering discussions. In what might be viewed a "consumer model," we gave the customer what the customer wanted in the hope he would be more motivated to return to the store.

Our effort to negotiate the curriculum went well beyond the steps just outlined. Our pre-ART assessment battery always included the Skillstreaming Skill Checklist (Goldstein et al., 1980; Goldstein & McGinnis, 1997), a listing of the 50 skills along with a brief definition of each and a five-point response scale ranging from "never" to "almost always" for rating frequency of correct use. We employed three separate versions of this measure, one each for staff, parents, and participating youths. Thus, in the community-based study, each youth completed one checklist on himself, indicating his current correct use of each of the 50 skills.

When the youths arrived for their initial ART session, posted at the front of the room was a large chart resembling Table 5.1. After brief introductions, the trainer said to the group:

> I'd like you to take a good look at this chart. Do you remember the skill checklist we gave you last week? Well, Susan and I have done a tally of your answers. Do you know what a tally is? We took everyone's answers and combined them so we could see how many of you eight felt you now correctly use each skill. Now look at this *(pointing)*. Six of you chose Dealing with an Accusation as a skill you hardly ever use well. So that's the one we'll teach you first.

In addition to skill negotiation before and at the first meeting, we sought to empower the youth via additional incarnations of this strategy. In the example, the first skill taught was Dealing with an Accusation. The second skill taught was selected by the group's two trainers. After the youths had completed the skill, the next ART session began with a trainer's asking the group "How's it going?" or "What's been happening since our last meeting?" Out of the brief give and take prompted by these questions typically came information from the youths about readjustment to the community and difficulties at home, in school, on the street, at work, or elsewhere. Perhaps one youth described arguing with a parent about curfew, and a second had a run-in with an after-school employer about getting to work on time or job performance. We followed such problem identification with skill negotiation, in which we jointly selected one or more skills that fit the problem(s) identified. In the example just cited, the youths and trainers chose a skill they felt jointly was relevant to getting along better with someone in authority when a conflict arose.

We became advocates of client empowerment via curriculum negotiation. Pre-meeting, initial session, and subsequent meeting collaboration of trainees and trainers to select skills appeared, in regularity of attendance and subsequent study outcome, to have a substantial and reliable resistance-reducing and outcome-

TABLE 5.1
Skillstreaming Skill Checklist Choices

SKILL	NUMBER OF PERSONS CHOOSING IT
Dealing with an Accusation	6
Keeping Out of Fights	4
Dealing with Group Pressure	4
Responding to Anger	3
Expressing a Complaint	1
Responding to Failure	0

enhancing effect. At the heart of this strategy lies the option of client choice. With our secondary assistance, youths choose what they will learn. We have taken a similar choice-as-empowerment stance with the resistances that sometimes appear later in our skills-training groups, as the following dialogue shows (Goldstein, Glick, & Gibbs, 1998, pp. 121–122). Note, for example, the emphasis on choice in this exchange:

Trainee: This won't work.

Trainer: What do you mean, it won't work?

Trainee: Come on, get real, get out of that university, get out on the street more. You can negotiate up the wazoo in here, but you can't negotiate out on the street. Out on the street you got to hit the guy before he hits you.

Trainer: Now wait a second, what do you think we're doing in here? We're not teaching substitutes—we're teaching alternatives.

Trainee: I don't understand those words.

Trainer: All right, I'll give you a sports example. There's a team with a good quarterback, the only quarterback on the team, but for some reason, injury or whatever, one Sunday he can't throw long and he can't run very well. All he's got working for him is his short pass, and he's good at it. So on the first down, he goes out and throws that short pass, and it's good. Same thing on the second down, another good short pass. After the second pass the defense in the huddle says, "Two short passes on two plays—maybe that's all the guy's got today. Let's look for it." Third down he throws the ball short again, and the defense knocks it down. Fourth down, it's his only play, he throws it again, and they intercept it.

You're like that quarterback. You have only one play—your fist. You've got a fist in every pocket. Others look at you, you hit them. They don't look at you, you hit them. They talk to you, you hit them. They don't talk to you, you hit them. That's why you get into so much trouble. How about we help you become like a skilled quarterback, who has a variety of plays? You keep your fist, and if you need to hit someone, you hit them. I don't want you to, but I can't follow you around to stop you, and I'm not going to teach you how to hit. You're already better at that than I am. But keep the fist in one pocket only, instead of in every pocket. In the back pocket put a different play. It's called *negotiation*. We'll teach you how to do it, and as a group we'll figure out where and when it fits. Do you know that each quarterback is given what's called a playbook? It has all the plays the team can use in it, and it also describes—for each play—the game circumstances where that play fits best. So, let's learn the plays, and then as a group we can figure out when, where, and with whom the plays fit and should be used.

In the other back pocket is a miracle play. I think you'll call it a miracle play because once I tell you what it is, you're going to say to me it's a miracle if you can do that. But you know what? I've seen kids do it, and like any good football play, it fits some situations, and it doesn't fit others. It's called *walking away without losing face*. There are times adolescents like yourself can do it. Let's figure out together where and when. And in the fourth pocket, yet another play. So like a good quarterback you have a variety of plays.

Honoring the Client's Theory of Change

The client-empowering psychotherapies mentioned at the beginning of this chapter and my own clinical venture into the resistance-reducing utility of empowerment are described here as background to three works that bring the client empowerment philosophy to fruition. One is the work of DeShazer (1985), O'Hanlon and Weiner-Davis (1989), and Selekman (1993) on solution-oriented therapy. The second, to use the authors' terms, is "psychotherapy with impossible cases" as developed and described by Duncan, Hubble, and Miller (1997). The third is Bohart and Tallman's (1999) seminal work on client self-healing. Each approach relies on client choice, strengths, control, and empowerment as its basis for movement towards positive treatment outcomes.

Solution-Oriented Therapy

Much as Rogers (1957), Erickson (1980), and others before them have done, DeShazer (1985) has built his solution-focused therapeutic model on the core assumption that clients have within them the strengths and resources to bring about change in themselves. The approach concentrates almost exclusively on what is nonproblematic for the client, what is working well—his or her strengths and successes. Techniques operationalizing this approach rely heavily on (a) identifying and expanding already existing instances in which the client's problem behaviors are absent and alternative positive behaviors are present; (b) imagining what, where, and when such positive, nonpathological behaviors might/will occur; and (c) minimizing client and therapist attitudes and behaviors that might be deleterious to such empowerment efforts. Solution-focused therapy rests on the following assumptions:

1. *Resistance is not a useful concept.* The client should be approached with the therapist's anticipating cooperation and collaboration, not the need to exercise power or control.

2. *Cooperation is inevitable.* Therapists should build rapport and elicit cooperation by using what the client brings to treatment (i.e., his or her strengths, resources, language, and, especially, beliefs about why the difficulties exist and how they might best be remediated).

3. *Change is inevitable.* "Change talk" is emphasized rather than "problem talk" as the therapist seeks to co-create with the client positive self-fulfilling prophecies. Past, present, and

future successes are emphasized; focus on past and present problem behaviors, minimized. "When" and "will" are used rather than "if" or "might."

4. *Only a small change is necessary.* The client belief fostered and strengthened here is that small steps can and do lead to major changes. A sort of positive, foot-in-the-door success can grow into major accomplishments via enhanced expectancies for change and an expanded view of one's self-efficacy.

5. *Clients have the strengths and resources to change.* Using past successes as models for present and future successes, clients are aided in accentuating their strengths and resources, rather than their problems and pathology.

6. *You do not need to know a great deal about the problem in order to solve it.* Again, the focus is on identifying the circumstances surrounding instances in which the problem is absent and positive alternative behaviors are in evidence. Selekman (1993) comments:

> Once important exception sequences of behavior and useful client self-talk have been identified, the therapist's job is to amplify this material through cheerleading, highlighting differences, and moving the client into the future with presuppositional questions. (p. 40)

> Presuppositional questions might include "How will you know when you would not have to come here anymore?" and "Suppose we ran into each other at a store after successfully completing therapy, what steps would you tell me you took?" (p. 62)

7. *Clients define the goals of treatment.* Clients are asked to provide a detailed description of how things will be when the presenting problem is solved, including who, what, when, how, and where.

Reflecting these core assumptions, therapist behavior in solution-focused treatment is, to wit, focused on solutions! Therapists may ask *miracle questions,* such as "Suppose while you are asleep a miracle happens, and your problem is solved. How will you be able to tell the next day that a miracle must have happened?" "What will be different?" "How will you have done that?"

With clients who are pessimistic and unresponsive to miracle questions, Selekman (1993) follows with *coping questions* (e.g. "How come things aren't worse?"). *Scaling and percentage questions* may be used. The client is asked in the former to rate his or her problem on a 1-to-10 scale, then indicate what he or she will have to do to be able to make a half-point improvement in a week's time. *Future-oriented questions* are particularly useful in and reflective of this approach (e.g. "If you were to show me a videotape of yourself after we successfully completed therapy, what kinds of changes would we observe?"). As Selekman proposes, "Future-oriented questions promote rehearsal of new solutions, suggest alternative actions, foster learning, discard ideas of redetermination, and address the system's specific change model" (p. 75).

Psychotherapy with Impossible Cases

In much the same spirit as the solution-focused group, Duncan, Hubble, and Miller (1997) undertook a rather remarkable treatment project. These therapist-investigators communicated to the many other therapists and referral sources in their community that they wished to be of help with "impossible cases." They offered "free, live-team consultations to therapists in the community who felt hopelessly stuck and wanted to bring their cases in search of new directions" (p. ix). Their core assumption was that "success can occur with impossibility when therapy is accommodated to the client's frame of reference and the client's theory of change is honored" (p. x).

Since "impossibility" and "resistance" appear on the face of it to be closely related constructs, it is of interest to note what Duncan et al. learned over the course of this 5-year effort to determine how impossibility, or a therapist's view of a given client as intractible, likely develops. Closely akin to the view of resistance as an interactional force to which both client and therapist contribute, Duncan et al. describe four pathways to impossibility. The first is a therapist-ascribed expectancy pathway:

> One reliable pathway to the impossible case arises in the anticipation of impossibility. Whether the experience is borne in simple trait ascriptions or by establishing a formal diagnosis, once set in motion, the set or

expectancy of hard going or poor outcome can be surprisingly resilient. . . . In effect, the person is made
equivalent to the characterization or label. (p. 4)

The bias of solution-focused treatment toward "change talk"
rather than "problem talk" is a means of creating with the client
an outcome-enhancing, positive self-fulfilling prophecy. Operating in this first pathway to impossibility is precisely the same
process in the opposite direction: "Failure talk," explicitly anticipated or surmised from difficult diagnoses or labels, helps create
a failure-enhancing, negative self-fulfilling prophecy.

A similar therapist-determined dynamic lies at the heart of
Duncan et al.'s second proposed route to viewing (and treating) a
given client as impossible—namely, "theory countertransference."
Here, the clinician's adherence and loyalty to his or her theory and
all it implies in how clients are to be understood and treated may
blind the clinician to seeing the strengths, resources, and positive
potential in the client. Duncan et al. stress that clients come to treatment with theories of their own about how their difficulties arose
and how best to remediate them. In a clear statement about resistance as interaction, they describe how the client's and therapist's
respective theories may clash on the route to impossibility:

> Clients hold their own theories about their psychology,
> difficulties, and life situation. . . . When their points of
> view are ignored, dismissed, or trampled by the thera-
> pist's theory, noncompliance or resistance is a pre-
> dictable outcome. To the therapist, the client begins to
> look, feel, and act impossible. To the client, the thera-
> pist comes across as uncaring, disinterested, or patently
> wrong. (Duncan et al., 1997, p. 8)

Doing more of the same is a third path to impossibility.
Duncan et al. propose that intractability is fed by the therapist's
persisting in an unsuccessful approach:

> For a difficulty to turn into a problem, only two condi-
> tions need to be fulfilled. First, the difficulty is mishan-
> dled (the attempted solution doesn't work). And
> second, when the difficulty proves refractory, more of
> the same ineffective solution is applied. . . . A vicious
> downward spiraling cycle ensues, with the original dif-
> ficulty growing into an impasse. (1997, p. 10)

In part, doing more of the same yields impossibility because the client is then seen as someone both presenting the original problem and failing to benefit in spite of the therapist's best efforts.

Finally, impossibility comes about because the client's goals for his or her therapy are overlooked, misunderstood, ignored, disrespected, and not actively incorporated into the treatment plan. Instead, it is frequently the case on the road to impossibility that the therapist's formulation of treatment goals prevails, perhaps singularly so. As Duncan et al. put it, "To impose agendas motivated by theoretical prerogatives, personal bias, and perhaps some sense of what would be good for the client, invites impossibility" (p. 11).

Derived from these conclusions regarding the processes leading to the assumption that a certain client is impossible to treat is Duncan et al.'s credo, communicated to the clinicians who responded to the consulting invitation:

> We would like you to consider treating veterans
> [Duncan et al.'s term for impossible clients] by allowing
> their frame of reference to guide your actions. Within
> the client is a theory of change waiting for discovery, a
> framework for intervention to be unfolded and inten-
> tionally accommodated for a successful outcome. Each
> client presents the therapist with a new theory to learn,
> a new language to practice, and new intervention
> applications to suggest. (1997, p. 19)

How might therapists implement this credo? By emphasizing client strengths and abilities, rather than deficits and liabilities. By highlighting client resources by inquiring about positive pretreatment changes and exceptions to the problem. By accommodating the therapeutic relationship to the client's perceptions and desires, much like Lazarus's (1993) recommendation that therapists be authentic chameleons. As Duncan et al. put it, "Accommodations emphasize therapist monitoring of the client's response to the process itself and quickly adjusting as necessary to calibrate therapy to the client's expectations" (p. 29). Perhaps most important, therapists can attend to client needs by accommodating the client's theory of change. This involves consideration of the client's beliefs, attitudes, and feelings about the presenting problem, as well as his or her opinions about its causes, treatment goals, and optimal means for reaching these goals:

> In our work we embrace the strong probability that clients not only have all that is necessary to resolve problems, but also may have already solved them, started to solve them, or have a very good idea about how to do it. . . . Questions that highlight previous successes and competencies and elicit the client's hunches and educated guesses encourage participation, emphasize the client's input, and provide direct access to the client's theory of change. (Duncan et al., 1997, p. 53)

Furthermore:

> Rather than reformulating the client's theory into the language of the therapist's orientation, we suggest the exact opposite: that therapists elevate the client's perceptions and experiences above theoretical conceptualizations, thereby allowing the client to direct therapeutic choices. (p. 32)

This said, working with impossibility, with "veterans," involves more than using strategies and tactics to empower them. Therapists are urged to *take their own pulse,* to pause and reflect when feeling anxious about the client, pessimistic, urgent, or overly responsible for client change—each of which can feed a perception of impossibility. Therapists are also encouraged to *avoid attribution creep,* the self-fulfilling tendency for one's theory, diagnosis, stereotypes, and expectations to involve perceptions of pathology and prognoses of impossibility. To aid the therapist in this regard, it is recommended that he or she *cultivate a beginner's mind.* No matter how many clients with a given presenting complaint one has seen, for the "beginner," the case is new. It is, furthermore, crucial to *preserve the client's dignity.* Veterans, by the time of their third, or fifth, or eighth unsuccessful therapy, are typically both reactant to control by others and pessimistic as to prognosis. It is better for the therapist to see and internally process the client as a veteran, rather than as a resistant, chronic, impossible multiple-treatment failure.

Duncan et al.'s (1997) impossibility project is a daring effort. They solicited clients seen as the worst, prognostically poorest, and built a philosophy, a therapeutic strategy, and an array of treatment tactics deeply reflective of their confidence in client empowerment. Their program is a major step forward in both resistance reduction and minimization.

Self-Healing

Bohart and Tallman (1999) built on the Duncan et al. (1997) program in their empowerment-enhancing treatise on self-healing. As in the latters' work, therapists are viewed in a less traditional role. Rather than treat or intervene, the therapist aids and encourages the client's self-healing potential by acting as a provider of resources, information, ideas, strategies, and support. He or she functions as a facilitator, coach, or mentor. The therapist-client relationship optimally functions as a context or workspace in which the client more readily self-heals. Ideally, the therapy forms a backdrop that augments the client's ability to be creative and generative, explore and discover, and make mistakes and grow from them. As Bohart and Tallman note:

> Looking at the relationship from the standpoint of an active self-healing client . . . the relationship is most basically helpful because it provides a good workspace. It provides a safe, sheltered space within which clients can take a deep breath, step back, consider their problems in context, brainstorm with another human being, gain perspective, feel free to look at all sides, make mistakes, generate alternatives, reexperience old wounds and problematic issues, and find the strength to reconfront and try new things out. (p. 112)

> People will be more spontaneously able to grow through their own resistances and avoidance if they have a relatively safe and respectful environment, in which they feel safe to experiment. (p. 153)

In this self-healing approach, the client is viewed as a cotherapist, and the therapeutic process is conceptualized as an attempt at intelligent conversation between two interested parties: Objections by the client are seen as part of the necessary and desired give and take of such problem-solving conversation and not as resistance. Each party listens to and is influenced by the other, with the therapist viewed as an expert on facilitation and the client viewed as an expert on himself or herself. As the authors put it, "We recognize that the locus of power to cause therapeutic change resides in the client, and we need the client's active collaboration and input. We do not just want compliance with a treatment regimen" (Bohart & Tallman, 1999, p. 225).

In the self-healing perspective, client resistance may spring from a variety of sources. The client may disagree with the therapist philosophically, or a recommended course of action may seem unwise to the client. The client may misunderstand the therapist's rationale or recommendations, or understand but feel unable to do what has been recommended. The client may feel discouraged and demoralized or may wonder why he or she should change something that has at least brought some predictability to life. To all such sources and manifestations of resistance, self-healing seeks to take a client-empowering stance. Bohart and Tallman state:

> We want to reiterate the implicit proactivity in most cases of resistance. People try to solve problems from within their point of view. They may resist solutions offered from outside if those solutions do not fit their view of the problem, or if the solution threatens the whole set of connections and interrelationships they have established in their personal worlds. . . . Thought of this way, resistance is a perfectly sensible reaction from the standpoint of the client. Because our primary job as therapists is to create a good learning climate, we must find a way to get clients interested and involved. . . . First, we need to show that we respect their desire to avoid us and to defend themselves against us. (1999, pp. 260–261)

Thus far, I have examined the contemporary work of Bohart and Tallman (1999); Duncan, Hubble, and Miller (1997); DeShazer (1985), O'Hanlon and Weiner-Davis (1989), and Selekman (1993). Other clinicians and investigators have also explicitly championed the resistance-reducing and outcome-enhancing value of client empowerment (e.g., Held, 1991; Kottler, 1992). Client empowerment is a respectful, collaborative, optimistic treatment strategy well worth further consideration, elaboration, and evaluation.

This chapter began with the important distinction between client empowerment as an outcome goal of all therapies and client empowerment as an in-therapy process strategy, a strategy characteristic of relatively few therapies. Following the examination of this small number of empowerment-process approaches, the chapter concludes with a look at one final approach. Its philosophical roots and treatment tactics are rather different from the approaches already presented, but its client-empowerment intent is the same. This is the cognitive-behavioral approach typically termed *self-regulation.*

SELF-REGULATION

In self-regulation, the intervenor serves as an instructor who teaches self-management skills and encourages their correct and continued use, while the client is his or her own intervention agent. If the "self-regulation instructor" is sufficiently skilled, the client develops a high level of understanding of the self-management strategy and rationale, high levels of competence in applying self-management tactics where and when needed on a continuing basis, and high levels of motivation to continue doing so. Introduction and integration of self-regulation philosophy and technique into the intervention mainstream grows from the pioneering work of Fred Kanfer and his colleagues (Kanfer & Gaelick-Buys, 1991; Kanfer & Phillips, 1990; Kanfer & Schefft, 1988; Karoly & Kanfer, 1982). Their collective efforts form the basis for discussion of the following self-regulation techniques: (a) goal setting, (b) self-monitoring, (c) self-evaluation, and (d) self-reinforcement and self-punishment.

Goal Setting

Self-regulation begins with goal setting—that is, forming and committing to decisions about modifying excessive, deficient, or otherwise problematic behavior(s).* The nature, levels, frequency, and very existence of such behaviors are considered, as are alternative routes to their alteration. Kanfer and Gaelick-Buys (1991) distinguish between anticipatory and corrective self-regulation. The former is a rehearsal process, an imagined journey through

---

*This section appeared originally in my book *Lasting Change: Methods for Enhancing Generalization of Gain* (Goldstein & Martens, 2000). The topic is equally applicable here.

the self-regulation techniques described in this section. It is in these "thought experiments" that goal setting begins:

> First, a vague reaction to a currently unsatisfactory situation orients the person to a new goal. The person begins to think about a more desirable state of affairs, and motivation for attaining this state begins to build. As the goal is formulated more clearly, the person begins to examine, usually by imagery or thoughts, some possible strategies and pathways toward the desired goal. We have called this process anticipating self-regulation. (p. 312)

The translation of such imagined goals into action is the shift from anticipatory to corrective self-regulation. Initially, goal-setting decisions are made by the intervenor and client collaboratively. As indicated previously, the intervenor's task is instruction. If he or she is competent in this regard, the client's ability to frame his or her own goals will grow progressively, in a manner largely if not totally independent of the intervenor's guidance. Since at its core self-regulation is a client-managed attempt to achieve and sustain a given standard of desired and desirable behavior, the setting of that standard is the first step in the self-regulatory sequence. Progress toward goals provides both a feedback function (Am I progressing? Have I been successful?) and a feedforward motivation toward goal achievement. Optimally, goal setting is a motivating self-contract that simultaneously establishes an evaluative standard for goal accomplishment.

Self-Monitoring

Self-monitoring is the systematic observation and recording of one or another feature of one's own behavior. In the self-regulation sequence, one monitors aspects of goal-relevant behaviors. Kanfer and Schefft (1988) have noted that self-monitoring may prove especially difficult when what one is seeking to describe and record is not a discrete behavior or a specific, overt episode but instead a cognitive event, such as a hostile thought or a fleeting sense of being threatened. Self-monitoring has been shown to be useful for therapeutic purposes. Its reactivity or behavior-change function has been shown in a number of investigations (e.g., systematic recording of number of cigarettes smoked reduces the number of cigarettes smoked). Unfortunately, as a stand-alone intervention, self-monitoring results in short-lived gains. However, its therapeutic potential should not be overlooked.

Once it is clear which goal behaviors are to be monitored, therapist and client (or teacher and student) make decisions about how (e.g., wrist counter, recording sheet) and how often (e.g., as they occur, at given time intervals) the behavior is to be monitored. Self-monitoring is a skill that can be learned through customary skills-training methods. Schloss and Smith (1988), for example, suggest the following steps:

1. The intervenor clearly defines the behavior that will be self-regulated.
2. The intervenor explains the purpose of self-monitoring in the self-regulation sequence.
3. The intervenor models the recording procedure.
4. The target person role-plays the recording procedure.
5. The target person is provided feedback on the self-monitoring skill.

Self-Evaluation

The data generated through self-monitoring on frequency, intensity, or other aspects of behavior help the client evaluate his or her progress toward goal attainment. Goals can and often do change as a result of this ongoing evaluative effort. Negative self-evaluations tend to result in a lowering of performance goals or self-estimates of probable future success. Reciprocally, a sense of progress may generate heightened motivation and thus greater progress.

Self-Reinforcement and Self-Punishment

In the spirit of self-regulation, the self-evaluation effort should lead to self-determined and self-administered consequences. That is, the target person himself or herself stipulates what level of progress toward goals set earlier is worthy of reinforcement (or punishment). Ideally, the person will impose the selected consequences on himself or herself. As is true for consequences delivered externally, self-administered consequences may take many forms. These include provision or loss/withholding of tangible rewards, tokens, or points, and praise or criticism. Respectively, the individual might purchase a new item of clothing after losing 10 pounds, add (or subtract) points being accumulated to obtain a given material reward, or make self-rewarding or self-punishing comments like "I did fine. I'm making good progress" versus "Not much progress so far. I'm stuck and better work harder." As is true for externally administered consequences, self-administered rewards should progress from tangible items to self-appraisal.

The self-regulation sequence of goal setting, self-monitoring, self-evaluation, and self-reward or punishment, either as a stand-alone offering or part of a larger treatment package, has been amply demonstrated to contribute significantly to initial change efforts and to the transfer and maintenance of such change (Kanfer & Schefft, 1988; Lehr & Schefft, 1987; Schefft & Kanfer, 1987).

CONCLUSIONS

This chapter has journeyed through the topic of client empowerment, at one and the same time an old and new operating philosophy. Client empowerment is old in that it appears as a theme in a number of therapies originated many years ago. It is new in recently developed approaches that place client empowerment at the core of their rationale and procedures. As a good parent encourages a teenager to reach greater independence by respectfully listening and responding to the youth's need for autonomy and empowerment, so, too, these new approaches hold, should the contemporary psychotherapist listen and respond. Empowering the client does not disempower the therapist, however. Quite the contrary, according to the approaches reviewed in this chapter, empowering the client also empowers the therapist, but in new and different ways. Curtis and Diamond (1997) talk of substituting "power with" for "power over," a distinction I believe fits perfectly in this context. The therapist who shares power with, honors the theories of, and affirms the client may indeed prove to be an especially potent co-facilitator of client change.

CHAPTER 6

Counterresistance and Challenging Clients

This final chapter will explore and weave together two important themes. Both pose danger for the therapeutic effort and raise the threat of its failure. Yet both also pose opportunity and the possibility of contributing significantly to a positive therapeutic outcome. One is therapist counterresistance. Boredom, anxiety, threat, and fear growing from personal needs or history, theoretical preferences, therapist-patient cultural differences, and other sources may alter therapist perceptions, understandings, and behaviors vis à vis the client in ways that seriously impede therapeutic progress. Particularly challenging clients of different types, each in his or her own way likely to present high and continuing levels of resistive behavior, may similarly contribute to negative outcomes. To offset, or at least minimize, such therapist- or client-induced resistance, I examine here its sources and substance, and recommend means for its amelioration.

COUNTERRESISTANCE

Like so much else in the history of psychotherapy, forces operating to promote or retard therapeutic success were first pointed to by Freud. He observed, "We have noticed that no psychoanalyst goes further than his own complexes and internal resistances permit" (Freud, 1926/1959, p. 145). His recommendation to therapists to overcome their counterresistances was *evenly suspended attention,* a process similar to the free association asked of clients. As Schoenewolf (1993) describes it, therapists were urged to "counter–free associate." Reich (1933/1951) later distinguished between acute and chronic therapist counterresistance. The former is in response to and in interaction with a particular client. As Gelso and Hayes (1998) point out, acute counterresistance is in a sense situational, uncharacteristic of a particular therapist's stance toward clients in general. Chronic counterresistance, or what Schoenewolf (1993) later termed "characterological counterresistance" involves treatment-impeding perceptions and behaviors manifested across a clinician's caseload. To these two subtypes—acute and chronic (characterological)—Schoenewolf adds cultural counterresistance. Included here are political beliefs; religious beliefs; gender-associated biases; racial and ethnic stereotypes; and other perception-influencing values, projections, and perspectives.

Counterresistance may take several overt forms. Strean (1995) offers lateness, verbal inhibition, overtalkativeness, forgetting appointments, and more subtle behaviors such as avoiding certain topics and intellectualizing emotionally laden issues. Among others, Schoenewolf (1993) mentions avoiding eye contact with the client, forgetting a client's name, canceling sessions, falling asleep during sessions, denying feelings, avoiding confrontation, impatience, hostility, and appeasing. Strean classifies therapist resistances by means of the same five-category system employed by Freud (1926/1959), as discussed in chapter 1: regression and other defenses, transference resistance, epinosic gain, superego resistance, and id resistance. Strean has also sketched the manner in which therapist counterresistances vary by stage of therapy. From first contact, through initial sessions, to mid-therapy, and then to the termination phase, the therapist may in differing ways react resistively to client resistances; feel that his or her own qualifications or competency is being challenged; become anxious, threatened, fearful, or angry; or otherwise and in other ways display counterresistance. Behaviors such as these, though typically denied, are universal qualities displayed at least some of the time by all therapists. To say so is not to castigate the therapeutic community. Instead, it is a mere observation on their humanity.

Counterresistance matters, often a great deal, in determining the success of the therapeutic course. Schoenewolf comments:

> It is my contention that in most cases, therapeutic failures resulted not from the inability of analysts to analyze and resolve patients' resistances, but from their failure to analyze and resolve their own. Change and cure are brought about through the relationship itself. . . .
> Therapists must show through both word and deed

how a healthy personality functions; they must set an example for the patient by showing the patient that they are aware of their own resistances. Therefore, the first question the therapist must ask at every moment in a session is, "How am *I* resisting now?" (1993, p. xiv)

The contention that counterresistance is associated with poor therapeutic outcome has been empirically substantiated by Hayes, Riker, and Ingram (1997). The antitherapeutic processes by which this association takes place are hinted at in studies by Cutler (1958) and Bandura, Lipsher, and Miller (1960). Cutler found that therapists tended to respond defensively and avoid topic exploration when clients raised issues related to the therapists' own unresolved conflicts. Bandura et al. found that when clients expressed hostility, therapists with high need for approval tended to avoid the clients' expressed feelings or its bases. In short, counterresistances can and do stand as serious impediments on the client's road to a favorable outcome.

What is a counterresisting therapist to do? The standard admonition for those who wish to practice psychotherapy to also receive it is relevant here. The practitioner can and should make special efforts to examine his or her own behaviors, especially trying to discern negative feelings about a particular client (i.e., acute counterresistance), problems across different clients (i.e., characterological counterresistance), or difficulties with a particular type of client (i.e., cultural counterresistance). The energetic effort to be honest with oneself as a means of identifying and remediating counterresistance should be supplemented with regular peer supervision, regular consultation with a therapy mentor or supervisor, and, in some instances, dialogue with the client.

Just as is true for client resistance, therapist counterresistance is an interactional phenomenon. Both client and therapist contribute to client resistance. Both client and therapist contribute to therapist counterresistance. It is indeed a relationship duet. As Schoenewolf (1993) puts it, "It is an ongoing dance of resistance and counterresistance. You cannot have one without the other" (p. xiv). Beyond understanding the therapist's contribution to this resistance–counterresistance duet, it is useful to inquire what patient types and behaviors are most prone to evoke such therapist responses. Stated otherwise regarding the phenomenon of therapist counterresistance, who are the contributing, challenging, difficult clients most typically involved?

Challenging Clients

In this section I focus on the types of clients described in the literature as particularly resistant ("challenging," "difficult," "intimidating"). I do so both because of their likely role in therapist counterresistance, and because consideration of the difficulties they pose illuminates means for resistance reduction. I began this elucidation in earlier chapters by describing impossible, involuntary, and noncompliant clients. The discussion continues here as I focus on delinquent youth, other defiant adolescents, and various types of clients (angry, reactant, remote, abrasive, assertive, self-defeating, help rejecting, manipulative, and others), including those who differ from the therapist on the dimensions of ethnicity, culture, gender, or social class.

Delinquent Youth

In our decades-long practice and research applying Aggression Replacement Training (ART) with delinquent youth, described in chapter 5 in connection with discussion of the empowering effects of negotiating the curriculum, we have experienced a wide array of resistive behaviors. These are listed in Table 6.1 and briefly described in the following text.

Inactivity

Minimal participation involves trainees who seldom volunteer, provide only brief answers, and in general give trainers a feeling that they are "pulling teeth" to keep the group at its various learning tasks.

A more extreme form of minimal participation is *apathy,* in which nearly everything the trainer does to direct, enliven, or activate the group is met with a lack of interest and spontaneity and little if any progress toward group goals.

While it is rare, *falling asleep* does occur from time to time. Sleepers need to be awakened, and the trainer should inquire into the cause of the tiredness. Boredom in the group, lack of

---

TABLE 6.1
Types of Trainee Resistance

INACTIVITY
Minimal participation
Apathy
Falling asleep

HYPERACTIVITY
Digression
Monopolizing
Interruption
Excessive restlessness

ACTIVE RESISTANCE
Participation but not as instructed
Passive-aggressive isolation
Negativism, refusal
Disruptiveness

AGGRESSION
Sarcasm, put-downs
Bullying, intimidation
Use of threats
Assault

COGNITIVE INADEQUACIES AND EMOTIONAL DISTURBANCES
Inability to pay attention
Inability to understand
Inability to remember
Bizarre behavior

Note. From *Aggression Replacement Training: A Comprehensive Intervention for Aggressive Youth* (pp. 57–59) by A. P. Goldstein & B. Glick, 1987, Champaign, IL: Research Press.

sleep, and physical illness are all possible reasons, each requiring a different response.

Hyperactivity

Digression is a repetitive, determined, and strongly motivated movement away from the purposes and procedures of the intervention. Here the trainee feels some emotion strongly, such as anger or anxiety or despair, and is determined to express it. Or the material being focused on may set off associations with important recent experiences, which the trainee feels the need to present and discuss. Digression is also often characterized by "jumping out of role." Rather than merely wandering off track, in digression the trainees drive the train off its intended course.

Monopolizing involves subtle and not-so-subtle efforts by trainees to get more than a fair share of time during a session. Long monologues, unnecessary requests by trainees to repeat a step, overly elaborate feedback, and other attention-seeking efforts to "remain on stage" are examples of such monopolizing behaviors.

Similar to monopolizing but more intrusive and insistent, *interruption* is breaking into the ongoing flow of an activity with comments, questions, suggestions, observations, or other statements. Interruption may be overly aggressive or angry, or it may take the pseudobenevolent form of "help" to the trainer. In either event, such interruptions more often than not retard the group's progress toward its goals.

Excessive restlessness is a more extreme, more physical form of hyperactivity. The trainees may fidget while sitting; rock their chairs; get up and pace; or display nonverbal, verbal, gestural, or postural signs of restlessness. Excessive restlessness is typically accompanied by digression, monopolizing, or interrupting behavior.

Active Resistance

Trainees involved in *participation but not as instructed* are off target. They may be trying to present their perspective, role-play as requested, serve as a coactor, give accurate feedback, or engage in other tasks required in the given session, but their own personal agendas or misperceptions interfere, and they wander off course to irrelevant or semirelevant topics. As such, this problem behavior is related to digression, although digression is perhaps a more intense manifestation of off-task behavior.

Passive-aggressive isolation is not merely apathy, in which trainees are simply uninterested in participating. Nor is it participation but not as instructed, in which trainees actively go off task and raise personal agendas. Passive-aggressive isolation is the purposeful, intentional withholding of appropriate participation, an active shutting down of involvement. It can be thought of as a largely nonverbal "crossing of one's arms" in order to display deliberate nonparticipation.

When displaying *negativism* and *refusal,* trainees signal more overtly, by word and deed, the desire to avoid participation in the group. They may openly refuse to be part of a role-play, listen to trainer instructions, or complete homework assignments. Or they may miss sessions, come late to sessions, or walk out in the middle of a session.

Disruptiveness encompasses active resistance behaviors more extreme than negativism, such as openly and perhaps energetically ridiculing the trainer, other trainees, or aspects of the intervention's procedures. Or disruptiveness may be shown by gestures, movements, noises, or other distracting nonverbal behaviors characteristically symbolizing overt criticism and hostility.

Aggression

Sarcasm and *put-downs* are denigrating trainee comments, made to ridicule the behaviors of a fellow group member. The intent of such caustic evaluations is to criticize and diminish the appraised worth of such performances.

Bullying and *intimidation* are common problem behaviors, as they are modes often characteristic of the youngsters selected for participation in Aggression Replacement Training. We distinguish these problems from the use of sarcasm and put-downs in that the behaviors in this category are more severe in intent and consequences.

Continuing along the severity continuum, the overt use of explicit *threats* is the next category of group management problems. One youth may threaten another with embarrassment, revelation of confidences, or even bodily harm if his or her demands are not met.

Finally, on rare occasions, actual physical *assault* may occur in a group. This serious breach of group safety can have long-term negative consequences for group functioning. The negative implications for the group's skills training agenda do not easily dissipate.

Cognitive Inadequacies
and Emotional Disturbances

Closely related to excessive restlessness, the *inability to pay attention* is often a result of internal or external distractions, day-dreaming, or other pressing agendas that command trainees' attention. Inability to pay attention, except for brief time spans, may also be due to one or more forms of cognitive impairment.

Cognitive deficits due to developmental disability, intellectual inadequacy, impoverishment of experience, disease processes, or other sources may result in trainees' *inability to understand* aspects of the curriculum. Failure to understand can, of course, also result from the trainer's lack of instructional clarity or excess complexity.

Material presented in the group may be attended to and understood by the trainees, but not remembered. *Inability to remember* may result in group management problems when what is forgotten includes rules and procedures for trainee participation, homework assignments, and so forth.

Bizarre behavior is uncommon, but when it does occur, it can be especially disruptive to group functioning. This type of group management problem may not only pull other trainees off task, it may also frighten them or make them highly anxious. The range of bizarre behaviors possible is quite broad, including talking to oneself or inanimate objects, offering incoherent statements to the group, becoming angry for no apparent reason, hearing and responding to imaginary voices, and exhibiting peculiar mannerisms.

In seeking to alter these progress-inhibiting resistive behaviors, we have taken three complementary approaches. One has been to make regular use of behavior modification techniques to reduce their frequency and promote alternative, desirable (non-resistive) behaviors. Especially useful here have been behavioral rules, time-out, response cost, and, particularly, a catch-them-being-good emphasis on rewarding the positive. Second, since ART is in part a social skills training method, we employ it for resistance-reducing purposes. The problematic behaviors that are the concern of this chapter—minimal participation, disruptiveness, digression, bullying, bizarre behavior, and so forth—can be viewed as behavioral excesses to be reduced by one or more of the means already examined. Such behaviors, however, can also be construed as behavioral deficiencies (e.g., too much monopolizing is too little listening to others, too much bullying is too little empathy directed toward others, etc.). Thus, an additional means for reducing problem behaviors is to replace them with desirable behaviors. The Skillstreaming curriculum is made up of just such alternatives. These skills may be taught as previously scheduled, as part of regular sessions, or at opportune times (teachable moments) to help trainees reduce resistance and open up to learning other skills.

Finally, we deal with resistance by letting our "diagnosis" of the resistance help determine its "cure." As the ART session unfolds, trainees may display resistive behavior. One trainee starts engaging in rough horseplay with another trainee. In another group, when a trainee is asked to set the stage for an anger control role-play or to share her reasoning regarding a given moral dilemma, that trainee begins delivering a monologue about irrelevant matters. In a third group, a trainee laughs at another trainee's role-play and shouts demeaning evaluations of the effort. In yet another group, a trainee sits, arms folded and silent, shaking his head "no" time and time again as he refuses the trainer's request that he come up front for his turn at role-playing. We urge trainers to ask themselves *Why?* Why at this moment is the trainee engaging in this particular behavior? Trainers need to make a guess, a hypothesis, a diagnosis. Perhaps one's hypothesis is that the trainee is displaying the particular resistive behavior at that moment because what is being asked is too complicated (too many steps, too complex a challenge, too demanding a requirement). If so, resistance reduction would take the form of simplifying—decreasing demands on the trainee's abilities. Following are some steps trainers take during the Skillstreaming or anger control training component of ART to simplify what is asked of trainees when it appears that procedural requests are too complicated:

1. Reward minimal trainee accomplishment.
2. Shorten role-plays.
3. "Feed" sentences to the trainee.
4. Have the trainee read a prepared script portraying the behavioral steps.
5. Have the trainee play the coactor role first.

Alternatively, assume a different hypothesis for the behavior. Perhaps the trainer thinks, "No, it's not too complicated. Helen has handled even more difficult demands before. Perhaps she's feeling threatened. The feedback to Sarah from Charlie and Ed on her role-play was really tough. She had a hard time dealing with it. Maybe Helen is afraid she's about to become their next target." If, as in this example, threat and intimidation are the diagnosis, steps to reduce the threat must be taken immediately. Following are several suggestions for reducing threatening behavior:

1. Employ additional live modeling.

2. Postpone the trainee's role-playing until last.

3. Provide reassurance to the trainee.

4. Provide empathic encouragement to the trainee.

5. Clarify aspects of the trainee's task that are experienced as threatening.

6. Confront and reorient the sources of the threat.

The goals in seeking to reduce these problematic behaviors are straightforward: (a) to maximize the youths' involvement, on-task time, and potential learning and (b) to minimize the time spent in distraction, aggression, or other off-task behaviors.

Other Defiant Adolescents

McHolland (1985) recommends general rules for dealing with all resistive adolescents and a series of subrules depending on subtypes of resistive youth. The general rules are as follows:

1. Start the interview by requesting basic information—such as age, grade, school, favorite TV show, and the like—rather than by seeking problem-related material.

2. Avoid silences.

3. Allow the adolescent to talk without advising, judging, or interrupting.

4. Within appropriate, not too personal, boundaries provide self-disclosure.

5. Learn about the youth's presenting problem gradually, offering support and understanding generously as it is shared.

McHolland's (1985) general recommendations are augmented by those offered by Sommers-Flanagan and Sommers-Flanagan (1997). The latter correctly observe that therapy involving an adult therapist and an adolescent client is, in reality, cross-cultural therapy. They suggest that barriers to cross-cultural understanding can be overcome successfully if the therapist acknowledges his or her "cultural" ignorance, is open to learning about adolescence from the adolescent, avoids trying to reparent the client, tries to function as a positive model, respects the client's opinions, maintains a sense of humor, stresses confidentiality and informed consent, and, more generally, acts toward the client with respect and integrity.

McHolland (1985) groups such youngsters into four subtypes and suggests that one's resistance reduction strategies vary by type. Consider the example of client silence. The *coerced* adolescent is the involuntary client described in chapter 5, required to go to therapy by family, school, or court. McHolland describes this youngster as one with an attitude of "uncooperativeness, active defiance, or open hostility both in word and action" (p. 356). This youth's silence, it is recommended, may be dealt with by (a) relabeling it ("You are very good at remaining silent. I bet you had this planned. You do it well"); (b) prescribing it ("The best way you can cooperate with me is to remain silent while I discuss your problems with your parents"); (c) reflecting on the feelings of hurt underlying the defiance; (d) recognizing or acknowledging the youth's displeasure in coming; and (e) if necessary, scheduling a silent session in order to turn the silence into a cooperative response.

The second subtype of resistant youth, according to McHolland, is the *no-need apathetic* adolescent, who as in the previous example, has been coerced into a therapy that he or she professes by passivity not to need. The behavioral hallmark here is apathy and lack of anxiety, in contrast to the overt defiance of the coerced client. McHolland suggests for this youth a nonverbal interview, in which the youth is asked treatment-relevant questions but is instructed to indicate affirmative answers by "doing nothing at all," merely shaking his or her head for "no." The interviewer might ask, "You didn't want to come here, right?" When no response is given, the interviewer replies, "OK, good, that's a yes." Other recommended interventions are family sculpting; telling the youth that "I'll let others (e.g., family) speak for you"; and, as before, prescribing a silent session.

The *no-need anxious* youth is the third type. While also denying or ambivalent about problems or need for assistance, he or she displays anxiety, not apathy. Recommended here is acceptance of silence ("It looks like you need some quiet time to decide how you want help"), structuring ("Would you like me to ask questions?"), and utilizing nonverbal methods (e.g., family sculpting).

Finally, there is the *cooperative resistant* adolescent. This youngster acknowledges the need for assistance, comes willingly, and appears to be cooperating but does not follow through on treatment recommendations or treatment decisions. McHolland (1985) suggests that resistance in this instance is due to shyness, fear, or anxiety. It is best dealt with, he suggests, by asking questions, structuring the interview, or employing other anxiety-reducing procedures.

Angry Clients

It is perhaps with regard to angry clients, more than any others, that the resistance-counterresistance duet is most apparent. Anger begets anger. In the "easier said than done" realm is Matsakis's (1998) comment on anger:

> We are often taught that a client's ability to express
> anger toward us is a "gift"—a sign of trust. If clients
> don't trust that you're strong enough to tolerate their
> anger, open-minded enough to accept their angry self,
> and caring enough to continue to help them despite
> their anger, then they tend to keep their anger sub-
> merged, the thinking goes. (p. 1)

Yet client anger, Matsakis (1998) correctly notes, can at minimum feel like an attack on one's professional competency and at worst portend an imminent physical assault. No wonder it so frequently generates counterresistance. This latter fear is not baseless. Several sources report high and increasing rates of both verbal and physical assault on mental health personnel (Bensley, Nelson, Kaufman, Silverstein, & Shields, 1997; Hansen, 1996; Lipscomb & Love, 1992; Schneider & Marren-Bell, 1995; Soloff, 1987). It seems prudent for the therapist working with angry clients to behave not only therapeutically, but also with a modicum of self-protectiveness and an acute awareness of his or her own vulnerability to counterresistive anger.

Matsakis (1998) urges therapists to ask themselves whether the anger is directed at them personally or at them as symbols of something or someone else. Essentially, one must seek to discern the meaning of the anger. Does it reflect transference, shame, rage, fear, confusion, or another underlying issue? Does it have a purpose in the therapeutic relationship, to create distance, safety, or, perversely, closeness? The client's anger, he urges, should be examined like any other significant emotion, with questions into its sources, intensity, forms of expression, possible purposes, and actual consequences.

Simultaneous with uncovering the roots and understanding the functions of client anger, the therapist may seek to defuse it. This can be accomplished in a number of ways, among them communicating empathy, redirecting, reframing, displaying calmness oneself, distracting, and teaching relaxation.

Anger may be sufficiently central to a client's presenting picture that instead of being an affect to be dealt with before getting back to the topics of therapy, it becomes the main topic. This is the case, for example, in Feindler, Marriott, and Iwata's (1984) Anger Control Training. Partially based on the earlier anger control and stress inoculation research of Novaco (1975) and Meichenbaum (1977), its goal is teaching chronically angry clients self-control of anger. In Anger Control Training, each person is required to bring to each session a description of a recent anger-arousing experience (a "hassle"), which he or she records in a binder ("hassle log"). For 10 weeks the clients are trained to respond to their hassles with a chain of behaviors including the following:

1. Identifying triggers (i.e., external events and internal self-statements that provoke an angry response)

2. Identifying cues (i.e., individual physical events—such as tightened muscles, flushed face, and clenched fists—that let the client know that the emotion he or she is experiencing is anger)

3. Using reminders (i.e., self-statements such as "Stay calm," "Chill out," and "Cool down" or nonhostile explanations of others' behavior)

4. Using reducers (i.e., a series of techniques that, like reminders, are designed to lower the individual's level of anger—for example, deep breathing, counting backward, imagining a peaceful scene, or imagining the long-term consequences of one's behavior)

5. Using self-evaluation (i.e., reflecting on the response to the hassle by identifying triggers, cues, using reminders and reducers, then praising or rewarding oneself for effective performance)

Research evaluations of Anger Control Training strongly support its effectiveness in the management and reduction of client anger (Feindler, 1981; Goldstein, Glick, & Gibbs, 1998).

Reactant Clients

Reactance has been defined as the motivational force to restore lost or threatened freedoms (Brehm, 1966). Its primary behavioral manifestation is noncompliance with and resistance to interpersonal demands and expectations (Hunsley, 1997): If you inhibit my freedom, especially my freedom of choice, and even if you do so for benign purposes with the goal of my betterment, I may react to such inhibitions in a way that restores my perceived freedom. As Seibel and Dowd (1999) note, such a state of affairs describes psychotherapy:

> In mental health treatment, there are myriad opportunities for the arousal of reactance. Treatment is typically administered by an "expert" or "authority" who may be perceived as prohibiting certain behaviors, attitudes, and lifestyles (e.g., smoking, competitive achievement). Such prohibitions, whether implicit or explicit, may arouse reactance. (pp. 373–374)

Dowd and Wallbrown (1993) found reactance to be greatest in persons high on autonomy, dominance, and independence. In the context of psychotherapy, both Morgan (1986) and Seibel and Dowd (1999) found them to terminate prematurely, possibly as a reactance-driven expression of these same personality traits. Rather than fight the resistance or force the reactant client to do one's therapeutic bidding, many therapists have sought to join, roll with, or go with such resistance by employing paradoxical interventions.

Paradoxical interventions are therapeutic procedures that seem to promote the client's problem or resistance rather than reduce it. As Meichenbaum and Turk (1987) note:

> In a type of "reverse psychology," the [health care provider] instructs the patient to continue to perform the destructive or nonadherent behavior, often in an exaggerated fashion. Implied in the directive is the notion that engaging in the problem behavior will eventually enable the patient to eliminate it. . . . As Haley (1963) notes, accepting patient nonadherence is the hallmark of [paradoxical intervention techniques]. "It is difficult to resist someone who is agreeing with you! . . . Joining the resistance has the effect of sabotaging it by rendering it no longer functional." (p. 29)

Paradoxical intervention techniques have multiple roots. Some go well back to the negative practice work of Dunlap (1928) and the early use of symptom prescription by Adler (Ansbacher & Ansbacher, 1956). Dunlap proposed that paradox via negative practices works in two ways. First, when a symptom is prescribed by a therapist and practiced by a client, the previously uncontrollable symptom behaviors come under voluntary control. Second, with repeated practice the behaviors become subject to satiation and extinction. Kopp and Kivel (1990) describe Adler's related strategy vividly:

> When there is resistance, a "tug of war" is taking place as therapist and client struggle to move in opposing directions. To escape the impasse, the therapist "puts down his or her end of the rope," thereby acknowledging that the client's resistance involves a resistance to the therapist's attempts to produce change in the client. The "escape" occurs when the therapist aligns his/her movement and goal with the client's. . . . In Adler's [1964] words, "I know that if I allow it, he will no longer want to do it. I know that if I hinder him, he will start a war. I always agree." (p. 142)

A strategy similar to dropping one's end of the rope was espoused by the psychoanalyst Spotnitz (1969) in his techniques of "joining the resistance" and "mirroring," in which it is made explicit to the client that he or she has the right to resist. Other psychotherapeutic approaches that have employed this and a variety of additional paradoxical interventions include existential therapy (Frankl, 1959); transactional analysis (Wathney, 1982); behavior modification (Ascher, 1989); and, especially, strategic/systems-oriented psychotherapies (Erickson, 1965; Haley, 1963; Weeks & L'Abate, 1982).

A number of specific techniques concretize the paradoxical intervention strategy:

1. *Symptom prescription.* The client is encouraged or instructed to deliberately perform the problem behavior or symptoms, or even to do so in an exaggerated manner. This approach restores voluntary control and, for the reactant client, restores autonomy and independence by thwarting the therapist's instructions (reducing or eliminating the prescribed behaviors). Variations on this technique are requests by the therapist for symptom modification or symptom exaggeration.

2. *Restraining.* In this approach the therapist discourages or even prohibits the client from changing or suggests that change can occur but only very slowly or only after a delay. As is the case for symptom prescription, the reactant individual, motivated to do the opposite of whatever has been instructed, will often engage in the positive behaviors the therapist actually wants.

3. *Reframing.* The goal of this paradoxical intervention is to change the meaning the client has attached to a given problem, event, or situation. The example cited earlier of complimenting the uncooperative, uncommunicative adolescent by relabeling his or her silence as a positive act (i.e., "something the adolescent is good at") illustrates reframing.

4. *Implied choice.* Absence of a sense of choicefulness lies at the motivational core of reactance. This paradoxical method involves offering the client a choice between alternative responses, *all* of which are symptom reducing. Would the client prefer to cease the problem behavior this week or next, here or there, with others present or alone? The choices are all up to the client, but all choices lead to the same result.

5. *Declaring hopelessness.* Offered first by Selvini-Palazzoli, Cecchin, Prata, and Boscolo (1978) as a last-ditch means for

seeking therapeutic commitment from very resistive clients, the therapist "gives up," admits his or her and the treatment's failure, and suggests that treatment be terminated. Clients may respond by terminating or, paradoxically, they may move to greater involvement and participation.

Investigative support for the effectiveness of paradoxical interventions is substantial (DeBord, 1989; Hunsley, 1997; Shoham-Salomon & Rosenthal, 1987). In fact, meta-analysis reveals that for clients with severe symptoms consequences may be both longer lasting positive consequences and more positive than consequences for an array of other therapeutic procedures (Shoham-Salomon & Rosenthal, 1987). In evaluating outcomes, however, a distinction has been drawn between compliance-based and defiance-based paradoxical interventions (Tennen, Rohrbaugh, Press, & White, 1981). In the former, the therapist wants the client to follow his or her suggestions—to perform and exaggerate. As Tennen et al. observe:

> Compliance-based prescription is indicated with symptoms such as obsessive behavior, panic attacks, and various somatic complaints which seem to be maintained by attempts to stave them off. The idea is that by attempting to bring on the symptom, the patient can no longer struggle against it, and under these conditions the problem or symptom often dissolves or comes under voluntary control. Another use of compliance-based paradoxical prescribing is to make the symptom or problem into an ordeal, the continuation of which becomes more trouble than it is worth. (1981, p. 18)

In the defiance-based approaches, the therapist's wish is that the client not follow the suggestions, and instead react by doing the opposite. Here the therapist wishes for more, not less, reactance. Tennen et al. (1981) even propose toward this end that the therapist come on strong, eagerly persuade, oversell the intervention, minimize client choices, and exaggerate his or her own degree of expertness. While both types of paradoxical intervention find support in the evaluation literature, the compliance-based approaches appear to be on firmer ground. In any event, a broad conclusion appears justified. Whether based on case studies, single-subject designs, or even to some extent controlled experimental investigations, paradoxical interventions are generally effective with diversely diagnosed reactant clients.

Cross-Cultural Clients

Perhaps one of the reasons that all psychotherapeutic encounters, to a greater or lesser degree, include instances of client resistance and therapist counterresistance is that *all* therapist-client matches are cross-cultural. Some are cross-cultural in the traditional sense (e.g., an American therapist treating a client from China). Some are cross-cultural in a somewhat less obvious manner (e.g., the Caucasian-American therapist seeing a Hispanic-American client). Others are cross-cultural in a very subtle manner (e.g., the middle-class African-American therapist treating a lower class African-American client, or a female therapist treating a male patient of the same ethnicity and social class as she). Whether based on nationality, ethnicity, religion, gender, social class, or other factors, therapist and patient invariably bring to their encounter some, and often several, cultural differences. These differences, both obvious and subtle, can and often do serve to instigate client resistance and therapist counterresistance. If this issue can be anticipated, understood, and mitigated, therapist-client cross-cultural differences may enrich rather than hamper the therapeutic process and its outcome.

Elsewhere I have described the benefits of "appreciative programming" for resistance reduction, therapist-client relationship quality, and therapeutic outcome (Goldstein, 1999). In much the same spirit of client empowerment (discussed in chapter 5), appreciative programming is an intervention planning and implementation strategy that in its philosophy and operating tactics relies heavily on consultation with the client. Particularly because so much of the cross-cultural influence on process and outcome of psychotherapy is subtle, we (the therapeutic community) often do not know what we do not know and should ask the persons who may. I have great regard for the cultural-sensitivity enhancement training programs developed and evaluated by scholars such as Pedersen (1986) and Sue and Sue (1999). They and others have demonstrated that therapist awareness, knowledge, and skill in working with clients of differing backgrounds can be enhanced and therapeutic benefit ensue (Acosta, Yamamoto, & Evans, 1982; Lefley & Bestman, 1984; Wade & Berstein, 1991).

Nonetheless, as a therapeutic community we have far to go in this regard. In a study representative of many of those reported, S. Sue (1988) found that African-American, Latino-American, Asian-American, and Native-American clients each terminated after a single session significantly more often than did Caucasian-American clients. Similar attrition has been consistently reported for lower social class versus middle-class clients (Garfield, 1994; Goldstein, 1973). While such outcomes are likely multiply determined, it is difficult not to assign a major role to therapist-client cross-cultural differences. As Sue and Sue (1999) assert, "Therapy represents a primarily Euro-American activity that may clash with the worldview of the culturally different client" (p. 28).

Continued refinement of cultural-sensitivity training programs remains an imperative, and access to clients' worldviews and opinions about how therapy might optimally proceed is a second imperative. As in chapter 5's discussion of honoring the client's theory of change, here, in connection with appreciative programming, I make the same recommendation, although the client whose theory is being honored may differ from his or her therapist in ethnicity, nationality, gender, or social class. In my own career as clinician and investigator I have more than once been impressed by clients' thinking and wisdom about the forms treatment might profitably take. In *Delinquents on Delinquency* (Goldstein, 1990), for example, I arranged to have a national sample of incarcerated adolescents interviewed regarding their views of what causes delinquency and youth aggression and what constitutes optimal intervention. Table 6.2 summarizes their creative suggestions.

Helms and Cook (1999) affirm this point:

> In psychodynamic therapy, the term *resistance* has a connotation that clients are fighting the process of therapy, when in fact they may not be responding according to the therapist's expectations because the therapist and client have different expectations for the process of therapy. What may be interpreted as "defenses" may in actuality be cultural patterns of communicating. . . . The therapist should invite clients to discuss their cultural values regarding talking to others about personal and family problems, and their expectations about how communications should flow when it involves them and an authority figure. (p. 146)

TABLE 6.2
Delinquents' Perspectives on Intervention

Early adoption for unwanted children	Closing of housing projects
	Videos of incarcerated youths
School uniforms	Celebrity campaigns
Longer school hours	Less-biased police
Learning how to think	Delinquents as store detectives
Classes on delinquency	Vans to pick up truants
Self-esteem groups	Alcohol-free bars and dances
Pictures of the future	Psychologists at arcades
Earlier work permits	Rewarding nondelinquency
Counseling advertisements	

Note. From *Delinquents on Delinquency* (pp. 153–154) by A. P. Goldstein, 1990, Champaign, IL: Research Press.

Armed with client-generated insights and resultant therapeutic adaptations and modifications, the therapist may more readily proceed in a culture-sensitive manner. As Cullari (1996) aptly notes:

> Resistance is an interactive process, and tailoring therapeutic methods to match clients' needs seems to be especially crucial when working with culturally different populations. Behaviors such as lack of self-disclosure, a reluctance to reveal psychological distress, an avoidance of direct eye contact, or a loose adherence to schedule or time limits may need to be interpreted and dealt with in a manner different from the one you use when working with traditional White middle class clients. . . . Psychotherapists who work with clients from different backgrounds need to be flexible. They should accept the idea that individuals from other cultures may have legitimate values that are different from their own and that certain modifications in therapy may be needed. (p. 171)

Other Challenging Clients

A number of other types of challenging clients have been identified, not so much on the basis of formal diagnosis as on their manner of engagement or disengagement with the therapist and the therapeutic process. Substantial levels of client resistance are apparent in these clients, as is the substantial possibility of therapist counterresistance.

The *remote* client presents one such resistance-counterresistance example. This client, typically voluntary, may be quite withdrawn or seemingly quite involved in treatment but in each case makes little progress. The remote client persists in being inaccessible, unavailable, present in body but not in much more. The implications of such a client style for therapist counterresistance are profound. Travers (1990) observes that "the presence of such a patient has the ability to leave the clinician with feelings of shame around one's inadequacies coupled with resentfulness for reasons not entirely clear" (p. 3). Wissler (1990) adds that such clients "can stir helplessness, awkward inadequacy, boredom and isolation" (p. 17). Paar (1990) describes the situation in stronger terms:

> I get drowsy and irritable and wish I could stop sneaking peeks at the clock. I know damned well that he sees me do it, but I can't stop myself. I just have to look. Nuts, only 10 minutes gone and 40 more slow-motion minutes left. . . . I see myself pulling farther back until he is left virtually alone in the room. (pp. 27–28)

Duryee (1990) notes that such feelings of therapist impotence, inadequacy, and resentment toward the client who shows up but behaves passively, instead of as a "good patient" should, may evoke counterresistive acting out by the therapist. Therapists may engage in

> such ultimately treatment-destructive interventions as implementing a greater frequency of sessions than the patient's level of contact tolerance can sustain, referring for medication, or viewing the patient as unamenable to treatment altogether. . . . The therapist whose training has not helped him learn that feeling like a bad therapist (and tolerating this feeling) is often part of being a good therapist is apt to have an especially difficult time working with them. (p. 96)

Remote patients commonly carry such formal diagnoses as paranoid, obsessive, schizoid, or borderline. These are treatable clients requiring much tolerance and patience in relationship building and gradual, incremental processing of affect and mastery attempts.

A similar counterresistance challenge is presented by the *abrasive* client. Wepman and Donovan (1984) describe this individual as frustrating and irritating. Imagine, if you will, treating a client described as follows:

> The people we have perceived as abrasive tend to have a high need for human contact, but a fear of emotional openness and intimacy. Their behavior is abrasive not only in that it is wearing on others but also because it is relentless. They keep coming on without regard to the signals that others send them. . . . The characteristics mentioned here—hardness, insensitivity to external cues, and intrusiveness—begin the exploration of the abrasive personality. The tendency to disregard others and, in an autistic way, to steamroll ahead to keep contact, whether it is reciprocated or not, seems to be a cardinal characteristic. (pp. 12–13)

If the therapist can move beyond the client's abrasiveness, or at least put it aside, he or she will be better able to reach out and address the part of the client's ambivalence reflected in the need for contact. As Stern (1990) urges, one can then better address the underlying hurt and "focus the work on the injury and not the resistance" (p. 17).

The same advice fits the attempt to reduce resistance and enhance therapeutic progress in a number of other types of challenging clients. These include the *overly assertive* client (Teyber, 1988); those who function in a repetitively *self-defeating* manner (Ellis, 1984); the *help-rejecting* complainer (Yalom, 1970); the *window-shopper,* a sort of serial therapy terminator (Fisch, Weakland, & Segal, 1983); and the *manipulator* (McCown & Johnson, 1993).

Each of these client types characteristically displays a high level of resistive behavior, and each generates, and in part becomes resistive in response to, therapist counterresistance. Successful outcomes will be likely to the degree that the therapist avoids construing resistance as enemy and instead examines it, understands it, empathizes with it, views it as an inevitable dynamic of the therapist-client duet, and prescriptively employs resistance reduction techniques described in this book.

CONCLUSIONS

Therapist counterresistance and challenging clients go hand in hand in the sense that challenging clients appear to help generate the very types of therapist counterresistance that lead to difficult sessions and negative outcomes. The fault—if it can be called a fault—lies within both clients and therapists, as well as within their interaction. These respective resistances can combine to pose a serious threat to therapeutic outcome. I hope the discussion and suggestions in this chapter will promote awareness of this danger and thus promote more satisfactory treatment outcomes.

CODA

Resisting Resistance

For a variable with quite a long history and one that lies at the core of some psychotherapies and at least on the periphery of others, remarkably little has been written about the concept of resistance. Given that systematic research on psychotherapeutic processes and outcomes began in the 1950s, the paucity of research on the topic is even more striking. Perhaps the reason relates to its theoretical complexity or diversity of definition or difficulty of measurement. Or perhaps, as Jahn and Lichstein (1980) suggest, the meager amount of research is best explained by the nature of resistive clients themselves. By definition, resistive clients fail to show up for initial sessions, behave uncooperatively when they do show up, and tend to drop out early and disappear. Hardly the ideal research target!

Whatever the cause or causes, a very great deal remains to be learned about the genesis, sustainers, and modifiers of client resistance. Three investigative paths I believe are especially needed, and that may be especially productive, concern the *assessment* of resistance, enhanced understanding of its dynamics via a process of *extrapolation* from sister variables in social and cognitive psychology, and its *prescriptive* modification.

While resistance classification schemas of varying degrees of specificity abound, including several described in this book, reliable measures of resistance are in very short supply. Schuller, Crits-Christoph, and Connolly (1991) have made a useful beginning effort in this regard, and continued examination and evaluation of their Resistance Scale's psychometric properties seem well worth pursuing. Dowd, Milne, and Wise's (1991) Therapeutic Reactance Scale may be a valuable piece of a comprehensive resistance assessment battery, as may Keijsers, Schapp, Hoogduin, Hoogsteyns, and deKemp's (1999) cognitive-behavioral measure of client motivation. Also potentially useful is Robertson's (1988) semistructured assessment interview, which seeks information regarding client motivation for psychotherapy by inquiring into client self-expectations, reactance, and locus of control.

Assessment beginnings do exist. However, most of the research on client resistance makes use of available but perhaps less-than-informative criteria—for example, number of "no shows," premature dropouts, and sessions before termination. While such behaviors may be significant indices of resistance, they fail to capture the richly informative, subtle client and therapist behaviors that may delay, detour, or sabotage therapeutic progress. These behaviors should command our attention.

I had the very good fortune early in my own career of collaborating with Kenneth Heller and Lee Sechrest in an effort to bring social-psychological work on interpersonal influence to bear upon our understanding of psychotherapy (Goldstein, Heller, & Sechrest, 1966). This was an effort of extrapolation, one of the three investigative paths mentioned previously. Alexander and French (1946), Dollard and Miller (1950), and Shoben (1953) had each earlier on sought to draw hypotheses about and explanations of psychotherapeutic events from experimental psychology—the research literature on learning in particular. We sought to do so using diverse domains of social-psychological research as our extrapolatory base. As part of this effort, Heller plumbed both laboratory and field studies of attitude change, persuasion, and communication to offer a series of hypotheses regarding how the dynamics of these processes might operate constructively in the context of psychotherapy with resistive clients. Higginbotham, West, and Forsyth (1988) updated and advanced the Goldstein et al. (1966) extrapolatory effort, in their case with particular emphasis on the challenges of conducting effective psychotherapy in the face of therapist-client cross-cultural differences.

Now, decades later, I would strongly reaffirm the value of an extrapolatory research philosophy in general, with reference to resistance in particular. The nonclinical domains of interpersonal behavior that might be drawn from to provide new insights about resistance and its reduction are numerous and diverse. For the interested researcher and thoughtful clinician, I suggest research on such variables as commitment (C. A. Kiesler, 1971); persuasion (O'Keefe, 1990; Stoltenberg, Leech, & Bratt, 1989); attitude change (Cacioppo, Claiborn, Petty, & Heesacker, 1991; Petty & Wegener, 1998); attachment (Mallinckrodt, Gantt, & Coble, 1995); interpersonal influence (Heppner & Claiborn, 1988; Strong, 1968); cognitive dissonance (Axsom, 1989); counter-control (Mahoney, 1991); language (Ryle, 1994); attribution (Bell-Dolan & Anderson, 1998; Kirmayer, 1990); information processing (Liotti, 1987); and self-fulfilling prophecy (Archibald, 1974; Jussim, 1986). To repeat, resistance is a powerful dynamic in psychotherapy, research on its workings is scarce, and we have much to learn. It is my hope that reaching beyond clinical bodies of literature will help us derive new knowledge and new techniques.

Finally, a word about prescriptiveness. I have described this desirable quality of intervention efforts in chapter 3 and will not discuss it again at length here. A large number of forms of resistance and means for reducing it exist, as do a similarly large number of challenging, resistive clients. A demanding task in most therapies, resistance reduction will advance most expeditiously if the clinician assumes a differential, prescriptive stance when selecting the means to do so.

Some general guidelines for developing and implementing prescriptive programming have been provided by Hunt (1971); Klausmeier, Rossmiller, and Sailey (1977); and ourselves (Goldstein, 1978; Goldstein & Stein, 1976). Munjack and Oziel (1978) have done so with specific regard to resistance.

Perhaps it is obvious to assert that "one size does *not* fit all." Just how to go about choosing which resistance reduction means fit which challenging client displaying which forms of resistance remains a largely unanswered, yet immensely significant, question.

References

Acosta, F. X., Yamamoto, J., & Evans, L. (Eds.). (1982). *Effective psychotherapy for low-income and minority patients.* New York: Plenum.

Adler, A. (1964). The individual psychology of Alfred Adler. In H. L. Ansbacher & R. R. Ansbacher (Eds.), *Alfred Adler.* New York: Harper Torchbooks.

Albrecht, T. L., & Adelman, M. B. (1987). *Communication and social support.* Newbury Park, CA: Sage.

Alexander, F. M. (1969). *The resurrection of the body.* New York: Dell.

Alexander, F. M., & French, T. M. (1946). *Psychoanalytic therapy.* New York: Ronald Press.

Alexander, R., Jr. (1997). Juvenile delinquency and social work practice. In C A. McNeese & A. R. Roberts (Eds.), *Policy and practice in the justice system.* Chicago: Nelson-Hall.

American Psychiatric Association. (1994). *Forced into treatment: The role of coercion in clinical practice.* Washington, DC: American Psychiatric Press.

Anderson, C. M., & Stewart, S. (1983). *Mastering resistance: A practical guide to family therapy.* New York: Guilford.

Anderson, R. J., & Kirk, L. M. (1982). Methods of improving patient compliance in chronic disease states. *Archives of Internal Medicine, 142,* 1673–1675.

Ansbacher, H., & Ansbacher, R. (1956). *The individual psychology of Alfred Adler.* New York: Basic.

Archibald, W. P. (1974). Alternative explanations for self-fulfilling prophecies. *Psychological Bulletin, 81,* 74–84.

Ary, D. V., Toobert, D., Wilson, W., & Glasgow, R. E. (1986). Patient perspective on factors contributing to nonadherence to diabetes regimen. *Diabetes Care, 9,* 168–172.

Ascher, L. M. (1989). *Therapeutic paradox.* New York: Guilford.

Atkinson, D. R., & Carskeddon, G. (1975). A prestigious introduction, psychological jargon, and perceived counselor credibility. *Journal of Counseling Psychology, 22,* 180–186.

Axsom, D. (1989). Cognitive dissonance and behavior change in psychotherapy. *Journal of Experimental Social Psychology, 25,* 234–252.

Baekeland, F., & Lundwall, L. (1975). Dropping out of treatment: A critical review. *Psychological Bulletin, 82,* 738–783.

Baker, E. F. (1967). *Man in the trap: The cause of blocked sexual energy.* New York: Avon.

Bandura, A. (1997). *Self-efficacy: The exercise of control.* New York: W. H. Freeman.

Bandura, A., Lipsher, D. H., & Miller, P. E. (1960). Psychotherapists' approach-avoidance reactions to patients' expressions of hostility. *Journal of Consulting Psychology, 24,* 1–8.

Baranowski, T., & Nader, P. R. (1985). Family involvement in health behavior change. In D. C. Turk & R. D. Kerns (Eds.), *Health, illness, and family.* New York: Wiley-Interscience.

Barofsky, I. (1987). Compliance, adherence and the therapeutic alliance: Steps in the development of self-care. *Social Science and Medicine, 12,* 369–376.

Barrera, M. (1986). Distinctions between social support concepts, measures, and models. *American Journal of Community Psychology, 14,* 413–445.

Bartenieff, I., & Lewis, D. (1980). *Body movement: Coping with the environment.* New York: Gordon and Breach.

Basch, M. F. (1982). Behavioral and psychodynamic psychotherapies: Mutually exclusive or reinforcing? In P. L. Wachtel (Ed.), *Resistance: Psychodynamic and behavioral approaches.* New York: Plenum.

Bath, K. E. (1976). Comparison of brief empathy training. *Perceptual and Motor Skills, 43,* 925–926.

Beck, A. T. (1976). *Cognitive therapy and the emotional disorders.* New York: New American Library.

Beck, A. T., Rush, A J., Shaw, B. F., & Emery, G. (1979). *Cognitive therapy of depression.* New York: Guilford.

Beck, J. S. (1996). *Cognitive therapy: Basics and beyond.* New York: Guilford.

Becker, M. H., & Green, L. (1975). A family approach to compliance with medical treatment: A selective review of literature. *International Journal of Health Education, 18,* 173–183.

Becker, M. H., & Rosenstock, I. M. (1984). Compliance with medical advice. In A. Steptoe & A. Mathews (Eds.), *Health care and human behavior.* New York: Academic.

Beitman, B., & Yue, D. (1999). *Learning psychotherapy.* New York: W. W. Norton.

Bell-Dolan, D., & Anderson, C. A. (1998). Attributional processes: An integration of social and clinical psychology. In R. M. Kowalski & M. R. Leary (Eds.), *The social psychology of emotional and behavioral problems.* Washington, DC: American Psychological Association.

Bensley, L. N., Nelson, J., Kaufman, B., Silverstein, J. K., & Shields, J. (1997). Injuries due to assaults in psychiatric hospital employees in Washington state. *American Journal of Industrial Medicine, 31,* 92–99.

Berlin, R. J. (1974). *Training of hospital staff in accurate affective perception of fear-anxiety from vocal cues in the context of varying facial cues.* Unpublished master's thesis, Syracuse University.

Berndt, T. J. (1989). Obtaining support from friends during childhood and adolescence. In D. Belle (Ed.), *Children's social networks and social supports.* New York: Wiley.

Bernstein, P. (1975). *Theory and methods in dance-movement therapy.* Dubuque, IA: Kendall/Hunt.

Berrigan, L. P., & Garfield, S. L. (1981). Relationship of missed psychotherapy appointments to premature termination and social class. *The British Journal of Clinical Psychology, 20,* 239–242.

Beutler, L. E. (1982). *Eclectic psychotherapy.* Elmsford, NY: Pergamon.

Blackwell, B. (1979). Treatment adherence: A contemporary viewpoint. *Psychosomatics, 20,* 27–35.

Blackwell, B. (1992). Compliance. *Psychotherapy and Psychosomatics, 58,* 161–169.

Blackwell, B. (1997). From compliance to alliance: A quarter century of research. In B. Blackwell (Ed.), *Treatment compliance and the therapeutic alliance.* Amsterdam: Harwood Academic.

Blatt, S. J., & Erlich, H. S. (1982). A critique of the concepts of resistance in behavior therapy. In P. L. Wachtel (Ed.), *Resistance: Psychodynamic and behavioral approaches.* New York: Plenum.

Bloom, B. L. (1981). Focused single session therapy: Initial development and evaluation. In S. L. Budman (Ed.), *Forms of brief therapy.* New York: Guilford.

Boczkowski, J. A., Zeichner, A., & DeSanto, N. (1985). Neuroleptic compliance among chronic schizophrenic outpatients: An intervention outcome report. *Journal of Consulting and Clinical Psychology, 53,* 666–671.

Bogden, J. L. (1982). Paradoxical communication as interpersonal influence. *Family Process, 21,* 443–452.

Bohart, A. C., & Tallman, K. (1999). *How clients make therapy work.* Washington, DC: American Psychological Association.

Bordin, E. (1994). Theory and research in the therapeutic working alliance. In A. O. Horvath & L. S. Greenberg (Eds.), *The working alliance: Theory, research, and practice.* New York: Wiley.

Brehm, J. W. (1966). *A theory of psychological reactance.* New York: Academic.

Brim, J. A. (1974). Social network correlates of avowed happiness. *Journal of Nervous and Mental Disorders, 158,* 432–439.

Brody, D. S. (1980). Feedback from patients as means of teaching the non-technological aspects of medical care. *Journal of Medical Education, 55,* 34–41.

Brooks, C. V. W. (1974). *Sensory awareness: The rediscovery of experiencing.* New York: Viking.

Brownell, K. D., & Foreyt, J. P. (1985). Obesity. In D. Barlow (Ed.), *Clinical handbook of psychological disorders.* New York: Guilford.

Brownell, K. D., Heckerman, C. L., Westlake, R. J., Hayes, S. C., & Monti, P. M. (1978). The effect of couples training and partner cooperativeness in behavioral treatment of obesity. *Behavior Research and Therapy, 16,* 323–333.

Brownell, K D., & Shumaker, S. A. (1985). Where do we go from here? The policy implications of social support. *Journal of Social Issues, 41,* 111–121.

Brunstein, J. C. (1993). Personal goals and subjective well-being: A longitudinal study. *Journal of Personality and Social Psychology, 65,* 1061–1070.

Bryant, B. K. (1985). The neighborhood walls: Sources of support in middle childhood. *Monographs of the Society for Research in Child Development, 50,* Serial No. 210.

Bugental, J. F. T. (1987). *The art of psychotherapy.* New York: W. W. Norton.

Bullmer, K. (1972). Improving accuracy of interpersonal perception through a direct teaching method. *Journal of Counseling Psychology, 19,* 37–41.

Cacioppo, J. T., Claiborn, C. D., Petty, R. E., & Heesacker, M. (1991). General framework for the study of attitude change in psychotherapy. In C. R. Snyder & D. R. Forsyth (Eds.), *Handbook of social and clinical psychology.* New York: Pergamon.

Cantor, N., & Langston, C. A. (1989). Ups and downs of life tasks in a life transition. In L. A. Pervin (Ed.), *Goal concepts in personality and social psychology.* Hillsdale, NJ: Erlbaum.

Capella, J. N. (1981). Mutual influence in expressive behavior: Adult-adult and infant-adult dyadic interaction. *Psychological Bulletin, 89,* 101–132.

Caplan, G. (1974). *Support systems and community mental health: Lectures on concept development.* New York: Behavioral Publications.

Carkhuff, R. R. (1969). *Helping and human relations.* New York: Holt, Rinehart and Winston.

Cassata, D. M. (1978). Health communication theory and research: An overview of the communication specialist interface. In D. Nimmo (Ed.), *Communication yearbook II.* New York: ICA.

Cervone, D., & Scott, W. D. (1995). Self-efficacy theory of behavioral change: Foundations, conceptual issues, and therapeutic implications. In W. O'Donohue & L. Krasner (Eds.), *Theories of behavior therapy: Exploring behavior change.* Washington, DC: American Psychological Association.

Chamberlain, P., Patterson, G., Reid, J., Kavanagh, K., & Forgatch, M. (1984). Observation of client resistance. *Behavior Therapy, 15,* 144–155.

Cobb, S. (1976). Social support as a moderator of life stress. *Psychosomatic Medicine, 38,* 300–314.

Coelho, R. J. (1984). Self-efficacy and cessation of smoking. *Psychological Reports, 54,* 309–310.

Coleman, V. R. (1985). Physician behavior and compliance. *Journal of Hypertension, 3,* 69–71.

Colletti, G., & Brownell, K. D. (1982). The physical and emotional benefits of social support: Applications to obesity, smoking and alcoholism. In M. Hersen, R. M. Eisler, & P. M. Miller (Eds.), *Progress in behavior modification* (Vol. 16). New York: Academic.

Collingswood, T. R. (1971). Retention and retraining of interpersonal communication skills. *Journal of Clinical Psychology, 27,* 294–296.

Condon, J. W., & Crano, W. D. (1988). Inferred evaluation and the relation between attitude similarity and interpersonal attraction. *Journal of Personality and Social Psychology, 54,* 789–797.

Corrigan, J. D., Dell, D. M., Lewis, K. N., & Schmidt, L. D. (1980). Counseling as social influence process: A review. *Journal of Counseling Psychology, 27,* 395–441.

Cullari, S. (1996). *Treatment resistance: A guide for practitioners.* Boston: Allyn and Bacon.

Curtis, L. C., & Diamond, R. (1997). Power and coercion in mental health practice. In B. Blackwell (Ed.), *Treatment compliance and the therapeutic alliance.* Amsterdam: Harwood Academic.

Cutler, R. L. (1958). Countertransference effects in psychotherapy. *Journal of Consulting Psychology, 22,* 349–356.

D'Alessio, G. (1968). The concurrent use of behavior modification and psychotherapy. *Psychotherapy: Theory, Research and Practice, 5,* 154–159.

Danish, S., & Brodsky, S. L. (1970). Training police in emotional control and awareness. *American Psychologist, 24,* 368–369.

Davis, J. R., & Glaros, A. G. (1986). Relapse prevention and smoking cessation. *Addictive Behaviors, 11,* 105–114.

Davis, M. (1973). Clinical implications of body movement research. *International Mental Health Research Newsletter, 15,* 1–7.

Davison, G. (1973). Counter-control in behavior modification. In L. Hamerlynck, L. Hand, & E. Mash (Eds.), *Behavioral change: Methodology, concepts, and practice.* Champaign, IL: Research Press.

DeBord, J. B. (1989). Paradoxical interventions: A review of the recent literature. *Journal of Counseling and Development, 67,* 394–398.

Dell, D. M., & Schmidt, L. D. (1976). Behavioral cues to counselor expertness. *Journal of Counseling Psychology, 23,* 197–201.

DePaulo, B. M., Zuckerman, M., & Rosenthal, R. (1980). Humans as lie detectors. *Journal of Communication, 30,* 129–139.

Derlega, V. J., & Chaikin, A. L. (1975). *Sharing intimacy.* Englewood Cliffs, NJ: Prentice Hall.

DeShazer, S. (1985). *Keys to solution in brief therapy.* New York: W. W. Norton.

DeVoge, J. T., & Beck, S. (1978). The therapist-client relationship in behavior therapy. *Progress in Behavior Modification, 6,* 203–248.

DiClemente, C. C., Prochaska, J. O., Fairhurst, S. K., Velicer, W. F., Valasquez, M. M., & Rossi, J. S. (1991). The process of smoking cessation: An analysis of precontemplation, contemplation, and preparation stages of change. *Journal of Consulting and Clinical Psychology, 59,* 293–304.

DiMatteo, M. R. (1979). A social-psychological analysis of physician-patient rapport: Toward a science of the art of medicine. *Journal of Social Issues, 35,* 12–33.

DiMatteo, M. R., & DiNicola, D. D. (1982). *Achieving patient compliance: The psychology of the medical practitioner's role*. New York: Pergamon.

Dollard, J., & Miller, N. E. (1950). *Personality and psychotherapy*. New York: McGraw-Hill.

Dowd, E. T., Milne, C. R., & Wise, S. L. (1991). The Therapeutic Reactance Scale: A measure of psychological reactance. *Journal of Counseling and Development, 69*, 541–545.

Dowd, E. T., & Wallbrown, F. (1993). Motivational components of client reactance. *Journal of Counseling and Development, 71*, 533–538.

Dowrick, P. W. (1983). Self-modeling. In P. W. Dowrick & S. J. Biggs (Eds.), *Using video: Psychological and social applications*. London: Wiley.

Dowrick, P. W. (1991). *Practical guide to using video in the behavioral sciences*. New York: Wiley.

Dowrick, P. W., & Jesdale, D. C. (1990). Effects on emotion of structured video replay: Implications for therapy. *Bulletin de Psychologie, 43*, 512–517.

Dunbar, J. M., & Agras, W. S. (1980). Compliance with medical instructions. In J. M. Ferguson & C. B. Taylor (Eds.), *Comprehensive handbook of behavioral medicine* (Vol. 3). New York: Spectrum.

Duncan, B. L., Hubble, M. A., & Miller, S. D. (1997). *Psychotherapy with impossible cases*. New York: W. W. Norton.

Dunlap, K. (1928). Revision of the fundamental law of habit formation. *Science, 67*, 360–362.

Dunlap, K. (1932). *Habits: Their making and unmaking*. New York: Liveright.

Duryee, J. (1990). So far, yet so near: Work with the remote patient as a close encounter in disguise. In J. A. Travers (Ed.), *Psychotherapy and the abrasive patient*. New York: Haworth.

Edelman, E., & Goldstein, A. P. (1984). Prescriptive relationship levels for juvenile delinquents in a psychotherapy analog. *Aggressive Behavior, 10*, 269–278.

Egan, G. (1976). *Interpersonal living*. Monterey, CA: Brooks/Cole.

Eisenthal, S., Emery, R., Lazare, A., & Udin, H. (1979). Adherence and the negotiated approach to patienthood. *Archives of General Psychiatry, 36*, 393–398.

Ekman, P. (1965). Communication through non-verbal behavior: A source of information about an interpersonal relationship. In S. S. Tomkins & C. E. Izard (Eds.), *Affect, cognition and personality*. New York: Springer.

Ekman, P. (1972). Universal and cultural differences in facial expressions of emotions. In J. Cole (Ed.), *Nebraska Symposium on Motivation* (Vol. 19). Lincoln: University of Nebraska Press.

Ekman, P., & Friesen, W. V. (1969). Nonverbal leakage and cues to deception. *Psychiatry, 32*, 88–106.

Ellis, A. (1984). Treating the abrasive client with Rational-Emotive Therapy (RET). In E. M. Stern (Ed.), *Psychotherapy and the abrasive patient*. New York: Haworth.

Ellis, A. (1985). *Overcoming resistance*. New York: Springer.

Emmons, R. A. (1993). *The psychology of ultimate concerns*. New York: Guilford.

Epstein, L. H., & Cluss, P. A. (1982). A behavioral medicine perspective on adherence to long-term medical regimens. *Journal of Consulting and Clinical Psychology, 50,* 960–971.

Epstein, L. H., Figueroa, J., Farkas, G. M., & Beck, S. (1981). The short-term effects of feedback on accuracy of urine glucose determinants in insulin-dependent diabetic children. *Behavior Therapy, 12,* 560–564.

Epstein, L. H., & Masek, B. J. (1978). Behavioral control of medicine compliance. *Journal of Applied Behavior Analysis, 11,* 1–9.

Erickson, F., & Shultz, J. (1982). *The counselor as gatekeeper: Social interaction in interviews*. New York: Academic.

Erickson, M. H. (1965). A hypnotic technique for resistant patients: The patient, the technique, and its rationale and field experiments. *Journal of Clinical Hypnosis, 7,* 8–32.

Erickson, M. H. (1980). The use of symptoms as an integral part of therapy. In E. L. Rossi (Ed.), *The collected papers of Milton H. Erickson*. New York: Irvington.

Fairbanks, L. A., McGuire, M. T., & Harris, C. J. (1982). Nonverbal interaction of patients and therapists during psychiatric interviews. *Journal of Abnormal Psychology, 91,* 109–119.

Feindler, E. L.(1981). *The art of self control*. Unpublished manuscript, Adelphi University, Garden City, NY.

Feindler, E. L., Marriott, S. A., & Iwata, M. (1984). Group anger control training for junior high school delinquents. *Cognitive Therapy and Research, 8,* 299–311.

Feldenkrais, M. (1970). *Body and mature behavior*. New York: International Universities Press.

Feldenkrais, M. (1972). *Awareness through movement*. New York: Harper and Row.

Fenichel, O. (1945). *The psychoanalytic theory of neurosis*. New York: W. W. Norton.

Fennell, M. J. V., & Teasdale, J. D. (1987). Cognitive therapy for depression: Individual differences in the processes of change. *Cognitive Therapy and Research, 11,* 253–271.

Ferguson, D. M., & Horwood, L. J. (1996). The role of adolescent peer affiliations in the continuity between childhood behavioral adjustment and juvenile offending. *Journal of Abnormal Child Psychology, 24,* 205–221.

Fine, R. (1982). *The healing of the mind*. New York: Free Press.

Fisch, R., Weakland, J., & Segal, L. (1983). *The tactics of change: Doing therapy briefly.* San Francisco: Jossey-Bass.

Fisher, E. B. (1996). A behavioral-economic perspective on the influence of social support on cigarette smoking. In L. Green & J. H. Kagel (Eds.), *Advances in behavioral economics* (Vol. 3). Norwood, NJ: Ablex.

Flaherty, J., & Richman, J. (1989). Gender differences in the perception and utilization of social support: Theoretical perspectives and an empirical test. *Social Science and Medicine, 28,* 1221–1228.

Ford, M. E. (1992). *Motivating humans.* Newbury Park: Sage.

Ford, M. E., & Nichols, C. W. (1987). A taxonomy of human goals and some possible applications. In M. E. Ford & D. H. Ford (Eds.), *Humans as self-constructing living systems: Putting the framework to work.* Hillsdale, NJ: Erlbaum.

Foreman, S., & Marmar, C. R. (1985). Therapist actions that address initially poor alliances in psychotherapy. *American Journal of Psychiatry, 142,* 922–926.

Foulkes, E. F., Persons, J. B., & Merkel, R. L. (1986). The effect of patients' beliefs about their illness on compliance in psychotherapy. *American Journal of Psychiatry, 143,* 340–344.

Framo, J. L. (1965). Rationale and techniques of intensive family therapy. In I. Boszormenyi-Nagy & J. L. Framo (Eds.), *Intensive family therapy: Theoretical and practical aspects.* New York: Harper and Row.

Frank, A. F., & Gunderson, J. G. (1990). The role of the therapeutic alliance in the treatment of schizophrenia. *Archives of General Psychiatry, 47,* 228–236.

Frank, J. D. (1991). *Persuasion and healing.* Baltimore: Johns Hopkins University Press.

Frank, S. J. (1977). *The facilitation of empathy through training in imagination.* Unpublished doctoral dissertation, Yale University, New Haven, CT.

Frankl, V. E. (1959). *Man's search for meaning: An introduction to logotherapy.* New York: Washington Square.

Freud, S. (1953). On psychotherapy. In J. Strachey (Ed. and Trans.), *The standard edition of the complete psychological works of Sigmund Freud* (Vol. 7). London: Hogarth Press. (Original work published 1905)

Freud, S. (1953). The future prospects of psychoanalytic therapy. In J. Strachey (Ed. and Trans.), *The standard edition of the complete psychological works of Sigmund Freud* (Vol. 11). London: Hogarth Press. (Original work published 1910)

Freud, S. (with Joseph Breuer). (1955). Studies on hysteria. J. Strachey (Ed. and Trans.), *The standard edition of the complete psychological works of Sigmund Freud* (Vol. 2). London: Hogarth Press. (Original work published 1895)

Freud, S. (1959). The question of lay analysis. In J. Strachey (Ed. and Trans.), *The standard edition of the complete psychological works of Sigmund Freud* (Vol. 20). London: Hogarth Press. (Original work published 1926)

Gantt, S., Billingsley, D., & Giordano, J. A. (1980). Paraprofessional skill: Maintenance of empathic sensitivity after training. *Journal of Counseling Psychology, 27,* 374–379.

Garfield, S. L. (1994). Research on client variables in psychotherapy. In A. E. Bergin & S. L. Garfield (Eds.), *Handbook of psychotherapy and behavior change.* New York: Wiley.

Gaston, L. (1990). The concept of the alliance and its role in psychotherapy: Theoretical and empirical considerations. *Psychotherapy, 27,* 143–153.

Gaston, L., Marmar, C., & Ring, J. (1989, June). *Engaging the difficult patient in cognitive therapy: Actions developing the therapeutic alliance.* Paper presented at the meeting of the Society for Psychotherapy Research, Toronto.

Gelso, C. J., & Hayes, J. A. (1998). *The psychotherapy relationship.* New York: Wiley.

Gendlin, E. T. (1981). *Focusing.* New York: Bantam.

Gendlin, E. T. (1984). The politics of giving therapy away: Listening and focusing. In D. Larson (Ed.), *Teaching psychological skills: Models for giving psychology away.* Monterey, CA: Brooks/Cole.

Gilchrist, L. D., Schinke, S. P., Bobo, J. K., & Snow, W. H. (1986). Self-control skills for preventing smoking. *Addictive Behaviors, 11,*169–174.

Glover, E. (1955). *The technique of psychoanalysis.* New York: International Universities Press. (Original work published 1928)

Goldfried, M. R. (1982). Resistance and clinical behavior therapy. In P. Wachtel (Ed.), *Resistance.* New York: Plenum.

Goldstein, A. P. (1962). *Therapist-patient expectancies in psychotherapy.* New York: Pergamon.

Goldstein, A. P. (1971). *Psychotherapeutic attraction.* Elmsford, NY: Pergamon.

Goldstein, A. P. (1973). *Structured learning therapy: Toward a psychotherapy for the poor.* New York: Academic.

Goldstein, A. P. (1978). (Ed.). *Prescriptions for child mental health and education.* New York: Pergamon.

Goldstein, A. P. (1990). *Delinquents on delinquency.* Champaign, IL: Research Press.

Goldstein, A. P. (1999). *The Prepare Curriculum: Teaching prosocial competencies* (rev. ed.). Champaign, IL: Research Press.

Goldstein, A. P., & Glick, B. (1987). *Aggression Replacement Training: A comprehensive intervention for aggressive youth.* Champaign, IL: Research Press.

Goldstein, A. P., Glick, B., & Gibbs, J. C. (1998). *Aggression Replacement Training: A comprehensive intervention for aggressive youth* (rev. ed). Champaign, IL: Research Press.

Goldstein, A. P., Glick, B., Irwin, M., Pask-McCartney, C., & Rubama, I. (1989). *Reducing delinquency: Intervention in the community.* New York: Pergamon.

Goldstein, A. P., Heller, K., & Sechrest, L. B. (1966). *Psychotherapy and the psychology of behavior change.* New York: Wiley.

Goldstein, A. P., & Higginbotham, H. N. (1991). Relationship-enhancement methods. In F. H. Kanfer & A. P. Goldstein (Eds.), *Helping people change.* New York: Allyn and Bacon.

Goldstein, A. P., & Kanfer, F. H. (Eds.). (1979). *Maximizing treatment gains: Transfer enhancement in psychotherapy.* New York: Academic.

Goldstein, A. P., & Martens, B. K. (2000). *Lasting change: Methods for enhancing generalization of gain.* Champaign, IL: Research Press.

Goldstein, A. P., & McGinnis, E. (with R. P. Sprafkin, N. J. Gershaw, & P. Klein). (1997). *Skillstreaming the adolescent: New strategies and perspectives for teaching prosocial skills* (rev. ed.). Champaign, IL: Research Press.

Goldstein, A. P., & Michaels, G. Y. (1985). *Empathy: Development, training, and consequences.* Hillsdale, NJ: Erlbaum.

Goldstein, A. P., Sprafkin, R. P., Gershaw, N. J., & Klein, P. (1980). *Skillstreaming the adolescent: A structured learning approach to teaching prosocial skills* (1st ed.). Champaign, IL: Research Press.

Goldstein, A. P., & Stein, N. (1976). *Prescriptive psychotherapies.* New York: Pergamon.

Goleman, D. (1977). *The varieties of the meditative experience.* New York: Dutton.

Gonder-Frederick, L., Cox, D. J., Pohl, S. L., & Carter, W. (1984). Patient blood glucose monitoring: Use, accuracy, adherence and impact. *Behavioral Medicine Update, 6,* 8–11.

Gordis, L. (1976). Methodological issues in the measurement of patient compliance. In D. L. Sackett & R. B. Haynes (Eds.), *Compliance with therapeutic regimens.* Baltimore: Johns Hopkins University Press.

Gottlieb, B. H. (1988). *Marshaling social support.* Newbury Park: Sage.

Greenberg, R. P. (1969). Effects of presession information on perception of the therapist and receptivity to influence in a psychotherapy analogue. *Journal of Consulting and Clinical Psychology, 33,* 425–429.

Greenson, R. R. (1967). *The technique and practice of psychoanalysis.* New York: International Universities Press.

Guenther, B. (1968). *Sense relaxation below your mind.* New York: Collier.

Guerney, B. G. (1977). *Relationship enhancement: Skill-training programs for therapy, problem-prevention, and enrichment.* San Francisco: Jossey-Bass.

Gumprez, J. J. (1982). *Discourse strategies.* New York: Cambridge University Press.

Guzzetta, R. A. (1974). *Acquisition and transfer of empathy by the parents of early adolescents through structured learning training.* Unpublished doctoral dissertation, Syracuse University.

Hafner, R. J. (1983). Behavior therapy for agoraphobic men. *Behavior Research and Therapy, 21,* 51–56.

Haley, J. (1963). *Strategies of psychotherapy.* New York: Grune and Stratton.

Hanna, F. J. (1996). Precursors of change: Pivotal points of involvement and resistance in psychotherapy. *Journal of Psychotherapy Integration, 6,* 227–264.

Hansen, B. (1996). Workplace violence in the hospital psychiatric setting. *American Association of Occupational Health Nurses Journal, 49,* 575–580.

Hanson, R. W. (1986). Physician-patient communication and compliance. In K. E. Gerber & A. M. Nehmekis (Eds.), *Compliance: The dilemma of the chronically ill.* New York: Springer.

Harris, G. A., & Watkins, D. (1987). *Counseling the involuntary and resistant client.* College Park, MD: American Correctional Association.

Harwood, A. (1981). Communicating about disease: Clinical implications of divergent concepts among patients and physicians. In A. Harwood (Ed.), *Ethnicity and medical care.* Cambridge, MA: Harvard University Press.

Hayes, J. A., Riker, J. R., & Ingram, K. M. (1997). Countertransference behavior and management in brief counseling: A field study. *Psychotherapy Research, 7,* 145–153.

Haynes, R. B. (1976a). A critical review of the "determinants" of patient compliance with therapeutic regimens. In D. L. Sackett & R. B. Haynes (Eds.), *Compliance with therapeutic regimens.* Baltimore: Johns Hopkins University Press.

Haynes, R. B. (1979). Determinants of compliance: The disease and the mechanics of treatment. In R. B. Haynes, D. W. Taylor, & D. L. Sackett (Eds.), *Compliance in health care.* Baltimore: Johns Hopkins University Press.

Haynes, R. B. (1976b). Strategies for improving compliance: A methodological analysis and review. In D. L. Sackett & R. B. Haynes (Eds.), *Compliance with therapeutic regimens.* Baltimore: Johns Hopkins University Press.

Haynes, R. B., Taylor, D. W., & Sackett, D. L. (Eds.). (1979). *Compliance in health care.* Baltimore: Johns Hopkins University Press.

Haynes, R. B., Wang, E., & DaMota-Gomes, M. (1987). A critical review of interventions to improve compliance. *Patient Education and Counseling, 10,* 155–166.

Healy, J. A. (1973). *Training of hospital staff in accurate affective perception of anger from vocal cues in the context of varying social cues.* Unpublished doctoral dissertation, Syracuse University.

Held, B. S. (1991). The process/content distinction in psychotherapy revisited. *Psychotherapy, 28,* 207–217.

Heller, K., Price, R. H., & Hogg, J. R. (1990). The role of social support in community and clinical interventions. In B. R. Sarason, I. G. Sarason, & G. R. Pierce (Eds.), *Social support: An interactional view.* New York: Wiley.

Heller, K., & Rook, K. S. (1997). Distinguishing the theoretical functions of social ties: Implications for support interventions. In S. Duck (Ed.), *Handbook of personal relationships: Theory, research and interventions.* New York: Wiley.

Heller, K., Swindle, R. W., & Dusenbury, L. (1986). Component social support processes: Comments and integration. *Journal of Consulting and Clinical Psychology, 54,* 466–470.

Helms J. E., & Cook, D. A. (1999). *Using race and culture in counseling and psychotherapy.* Boston: Allyn and Bacon.

Hendrick, S. S., Hendrick, C., & Adler, N. L. (1988). Romantic relationships: Love, satisfaction, and staying together. *Journal of Personality and Social Psychology, 54,* 980–988.

Henry, W. P., Schacht, T. E., & Strupp, H. H. (1986). Structural analysis of social behavior: Application to a study of interpersonal process differential psychotherapeutic outcomes. *Journal of Consulting and Clinical Psychology, 54,* 27–31.

Heppner, P. P., & Claiborn, C. D. (1988). Social influence research in counseling: A review and critique. *Journal of Counseling Psychology, 36,* 365–387.

Herzberg, A. (1947). *Active psychotherapy.* New York: Grune and Stratton.

Higbee, M., Dukes, G., & Bosso, J. (1982). Patient recall of physician's prescription instructions. *Hospital Formulary, 17,* 553–556.

Higginbotham, H. N., West, S. G., & Forsyth, D. R. (1989). *Psychotherapy and behavior change: Social, cultural and methodological perspectives.* New York: Pergamon.

Higgs, J. A. (1992). Dealing with resistance: Strategies for effective groups. *Journal for Specialists in Group Work, 17,* 67–73.

Hirsch, B. J. (1980). Natural support systems and coping with major life changes. *American Journal of Community Psychology, 8,* 159–172.

Hobfoll, S. B., Nadler, A., & Lieberman, J. (1986). Satisfaction with social support during crisis: Intimacy and self-esteem as crucial determinants. *Journal of Personality and Social Psychology, 51,* 296–304.

Hoehn-Saric, R., Frank, J. D., Imber, S. D., Nash, E. H., Stone, A. R., & Battle, C. C. (1964). Systematic preparation of patients for psychotherapy: I. Effects on therapy behavior and outcome. *Journal of Psychiatric Research, 2,* 267–281.

Hoffman-Graff, M. A. (1975). Interviewer use of positive and negative disclosure and interviewer-subject sex pairing. *Journal of Counseling Psychology, 24,* 184–190.

Horne, R., & Weinman, J. (1998). Predicting treatment adherence: An overview of theoretical models. In L. B. Myers & K. Midence (Eds.), *Adherence to treatment in medical conditions.* Amsterdam: Harwood Academic.

Horney, K. (1939). *New ways in psychoanalysis.* New York: W. W. Norton.

Horvath, A. O., & Symonds, B. D. (1991). Relationship between working alliance and outcome in psychotherapy: A meta-analysis. *Journal of Counseling Psychology, 38,* 139–149.

House, J. S. (1981). *Work stress and social support.* Reading, MA: Addison-Wesley.

Hunsley, J. (1997). Defiance-based symptom prescription and psychological reactance: A critical evaluation. *Professional Psychology: Research and Practice, 28,* 36–43.

Hunt, D. E. (1971). Matching models for teacher training. In B. R. Joyce & M. Weil (Eds.), *Perspectives for reform in teacher education.* Englewood Cliffs, NJ: Prentice Hall.

Ivey, A. E., & Authier, J. (1971). *Microcounseling.* Springfield, IL: Charles C. Thomas.

Jacobs, D., Charles, E., Jacobs, T., Weinstein, H., & Mann, D. (1972). Preparation for treatment of the disadvantaged patient: Effects on disposition and outcome. *American Journal of Orthopsychiatry, 42,* 666–674.

Jacobson, D. E. (1986). Types and timing of social support. *Journal of Health and Social Behavior, 27,* 250–264.

Jahn, D. L., & Lichstein, K. L. (1980). The resistive client: A neglected phenomenon in behavior therapy. *Behavior Modification, 4,* 303–320.

Janis, I. L. (1983). The role of social support in adherence to stressful decisions. *American Psychologist, 38,* 143–160.

Jay, S., Litt, I. F., & Durant, R. H. (1984). Compliance with therapeutic regimens. *Journal of Adolescent Health Care, 5,* 124–136.

Jennings, R. M., & Ball, J. D. (1982). Patient compliance with CHAMPUS mental health referrals. *Professional Psychology, 13,* 172–173.

Johnson, D. (1977). *The protean body: A Rolfer's view of human flexibility.* New York: Harper and Row.

Jones, L. K. (1974). Toward more adequate selection criteria: Correlates of empathy, genuineness, and respect. *Counselor Education and Supervision, 13,* 13–21.

Jussim, L. (1986). Self-fulfilling prophecies: A theoretical and integrative review. *Psychological Review, 93,* 429–445.

Kagan, N. (1972). *Influencing human interaction.* East Lansing: Michigan State University.

Kagan, N., & Schauble, P. G. (1969). Affect simulation in interpersonal process recall. *Journal of Consulting Psychology, 16,* 309–313.

Kahn, J. S., Kehle, T. J., Jenson, W. R., & Clark, E. (1990). Comparison of cognitive-behavioral relaxation and self-modeling interventions for depression among middle school students. *School Psychology Review, 19,* 196–211.

Kahn, R., & Antonucci, T. (1980). Attachment, role, and social support. In P. Baltes & O. Brim (Eds.), *Life-span development and behavior.* New York: Academic.

Kaiser, H. (1976). Problems in technique. In M. Bergmann & F. Hartman (Eds.), *The evolution of psychoanalytic technique.* New York: Basic.

Kanfer, F. H., & Gaelick-Buys, L. (1991). Self-management methods. In F. H. Kanfer & A. P. Goldstein (Eds.), *Helping people change.* New York: Pergamon.

Kanfer, F. H., & Phillips, J. S. (1970). *Learning foundations of behavior therapy.* New York: Wiley.

Kanfer, F. H., & Schefft, B. K. (1988). *Guiding the process of therapeutic change.* Champaign, IL: Research Press.

Karoly, P., & Kanfer, F. H. (Eds.). (1982). *Self-management and behavior change: From theory to practice.* New York: Pergamon.

Karpman, B. (1949). Objective psychotherapy. *Journal of Clinical Psychology, 5,* 140-148.

Kazdin, A. E. (1975). *Behavior modification in applied settings.* Homewood, IL: Dorsey.

Kazdin, A. E., & Mascitelli, S. (1982). Covert and overt rehearsal and homework practice in developing assertiveness. *Journal of Consulting and Clinical Psychology, 50,* 250–258.

Keefe, T. (1976). Empathy: The critical skill. *Social Work, 21,* 10–14.

Keeley, S. M., Shemberg, K. M., & Carbonell, J. (1976). Operant clinical intervention: Behavior management or beyond? *Behavior Therapy, 7,* 292–305.

Keen, S. (1970, October). Sing the body electric. *Psychology Today,* 56–61.

Keijsers, G. P., Schaap, C. P., Hoogduin, C. A., Hoogsteyns, B., & deKemp, E. C. (1999). Preliminary results of a new instrument in cognitive-behaviour therapy. *Behavioural and Cognitive Psychotherapy, 27,* 165–179.

Kelly, G. A. (1955). *The psychology of personal constructs.* New York: W. W. Norton.

Kerr, B. A., Olson, D. H., Claiborn, C. D., Bauers-Gruenler, S. J., & Paolo, A. M. (1983). Overcoming opposition and resistance: Differential functions of expertness and attractiveness in career counseling. *Journal of Counseling Psychology, 30,* 323–331.

Kiesler, C. A. (1971). *The psychology of commitment: Experiments linking behavior to belief.* New York: Academic.

Kiesler, D. J. (1966). Some myths of psychotherapy research and the search for a paradigm. *Psychological Bulletin, 65,* 110–136.

Kiesler, D. J., & Watkins, K. (1989). Interpersonal complementarity and the therapeutic alliance: A study of relationship in psychotherapy. *Psychotherapy: Theory, Reseearch, and Practice, 26,* 183–194.

Kirmayer, L. J. (1990). Resistance, reactance, and reluctance to change: A cognitive attributional approach to strategic interventions. *Journal of Cognitive Psychotherapy, 4,* 83–104.

Klausmeier, H. J., Rossmiller, R. A., & Sailey, M. (1977). *Individually guided elementary education.* New York: Academic.

Kleinman, A. (1980). *Patients and healers in the context of culture.* Berkeley: University of California Press.

Kleinman, A., Eisenberg, L., & Good, B. (1978) Culture, illness and care: Clinical lessons from anthropologic and cross-cultural research. *Annals of Internal Medicine, 88,* 251–258.

Klinger, E. (1975). Consequences of commitment and disengagement from incentives. *Psychological Review, 82,* 1–25.

Kohut, H. (1971). *The analysis of the self.* New York: International Universities Press.

Kopp, R. R., & Kivel, C. (1990). Traps and escapes: An Adlerian approach to understanding resistance and resolving impasses in psychotherapy. *Individual Psychology, 46,* 139–147.

Koss, M. P., & Shiang, J. (1994). Research on brief psychotherapy. In A. E. Bergin & S. L. Garfield (Eds.), *Handbook of psychotherapy and behavior change.* New York: Wiley.

Kottler, J. A. (1991). *The complete therapist.* San Francisco: Jossey-Bass.

Kottler, J. A. (1992). *Compassionate therapy: Working with difficult clients.* San Francisco: Jossey-Bass.

Krause, N., & Keith, V. (1989). Gender differences in social support among older adults. *Sex Roles, 21,* 609–628.

Kraut, R. (1980). Humans as lie detectors: Some second thoughts. *Journal of Communication, 30,* 209–216.

Kris, A. (1990). The analyst's stance and the method of free association. *Psychoanalytic Study of the Child, 45,* 25–41.

Kuo, W. H., & Tsai, Y. M. (1986). Social networking, hardiness and immigrants' mental health. *Journal of Health and Social Behavior, 27,* 133–149.

Kushner, M. G., & Sher, K. J. (1991). The relationship of treatment fearfulness and psychological service utilization: An overview. *Professional Psychology: Research and Practice, 22,* 196–203.

Laban, R., & Lawrence, F. C. (1947). *Effort.* London: Macdonald and Evans.

Lambert, M. J. (1982). *Psychotherapy and patient relationships.* Homewood, IL: Dow Jones–Irwin.

Lambert, M. J., & Bergin, A. E. (1994). The effectiveness of psychotherapy. In A. E. Bergin & S. L. Garfield (Eds.), *Handbook of psychotherapy and behavior change.* New York: Wiley.

Langs, R. (1981). *Resistances and interactions.* New York: Jason Aronson.

Larke, J. (1985). Compulsory treatment: Some practical methods of treating the mandated client. *Psychotherapy, 22,* 262–268.

Larsen, D. L., Nguyen, T. D., Green, R. S., & Attkisson, C. C. (1983). Enhancing the utilization of outpatient mental health services. *Community Mental Health Journal, 19,* 305–320.

Laundergan, J. C., Spicer, J. W., & Kammerer, N. L. (1979). *Are court referrals effective?* Center City, MN: Hazelden.

Lazarus, A. A. (1981). *The practice of multimodal therapy: Systematic, comprehensive and effective psychotherapy.* New York: McGraw-Hill.

Lazarus, A. A. (1993). Tailoring the therapeutic relationship, or being an authentic chameleon. *Psychotherapy, 30,* 404–407.

Lazarus, A. A., & Fay, A. (1982). Resistance or rationalization? A cognitive-behavioral perspective. In P. Wachtel (Ed.), *Resistance.* New York: Plenum.

Lefley, H. P., & Bestman, E. W. (1984). Community mental health and minorities. In S. Sue & T. Moore (Eds.), *The pluralistic society: A community mental health perspective.* New York: Human Sciences.

Lehr, B. K., & Schefft, B. K. (1987, August). *Self-management therapy versus cognitive-behavioral therapy in cardiac rehabilitation.* Paper presented at the annual meeting of the American Psychological Association, New York.

Leipold, W. E. (1963). *Psychological distance in a dyadic interview.* Unpublished doctoral dissertation, University of North Dakota, Grand Forks.

Lesh, T. V. (1970). Zen meditation and the development of empathy in counselors. *Journal of Humanistic Psychology, 10,* 39–74.

Ley, P. (1979). Memory for medical information. *British Journal of Social and Clinical Psychology, 18,* 245–255.

Lin, N. (1986). Conceptualizing social support. In N. Lin, A. Dean, & W. Ensel (Eds.), *Social support, life events and depression.* Orlando: Academic.

Liotti, G. (1987). The resistance to change of cognitive structures: A counterproposal to psychoanalytic metapsychology. *Journal of Cognitive Psychotherapy, 1,* 87–104.

Lipscomb, J., & Love, C. (1992). Violence toward health care workers: An emerging occupational hazard. *American Association of Occupational Health Nurses Journal, 40,* 219–228.

Little, B. R. (1983). Personal projects: A rationale and method for investigation. *Environment and Behavior, 15,* 273–309.

Locke, E. A., & Latham, G. P. (Eds.). (1990). *A theory of goal setting and task performance.* Englewood Cliffs, NJ: Prentice Hall.

Lopez, M. A. (1977). *The influence of vocal and facial cue training on the identification of affect communicated via paralinguistic cues.* Unpublished master's thesis, Syracuse University.

Lowen, A. (1975). *Bioenergetics.* New York: Coward, McCann, and Geoghegan.

Lowen, A., & Lowen, L. (1977). *The way to vibrant health: A manual of bioenergetic exercises.* New York: Harper and Row.

Luborsky, L. (1994). Therapeutic alliances as predictors of psychotherapy outcomes: Factors explaining the predictive success. In A. O. Horvath & L. S. Greenberg (Eds.), *The working alliance: Theory, research, and practice.* New York: Wiley.

Luther, G., & Loev, I. (1981, October). Resistance in marital therapy. *Journal of Marital and Family Therapy,* 475–480.

Macharia, W. M., Leon, G., Rowe, B. H., Stephenson, B. J., & Haynes, R. B. (1992). An overview of interventions to improve compliance with appointment keeping for medical services. *Journal of the American Medical Association, 267,* 1813–1817.

Maddi, S. R., Kahn, S., & Maddi, K. L. (1998). The effectiveness of hardiness training. *Consulting Psychology Journal: Practice and Research, 50,* 78–86.

Maddux, J. E., & Meier, L. J. (1995). Self-efficacy and depression. In J. E. Maddux (Ed.), *Self-efficacy, adaptation, and adjustment: Theory, research, and application.* New York: Plenum.

Mahoney, M. J. (1991). *The human change process.* New York: Basic.

Malahey, B. (1966). The effects of instructions and labeling on the number of medication errors made by patients at home. *American Journal of Hospital Pharmacy, 23,* 283–292.

Mallinckrodt, B., Gantt, D. L., & Coble, H. M. (1995). Attachment patterns in the psychotherapy relationship: Development of the Client Attachment to Therapist Scale. *Journal of Counseling Psychology, 42,* 307–317.

Markus, H., & Nurius, P. (1986). Possible selves. *American Psychologist, 41,* 954–969.

Marmar, C. R., Gaston, L., Gallagher, D., & Thompson, L. W. (1989). Alliance and outcome in late-life depression. *Journal of Nervous and Mental Disease, 177,* 464–472.

Marshall, R. J. (1997). *Resistant interactions: Child, family, and psychotherapist.* Northvale, NJ: Jason Aronson.

Masters, W. H., & Johnson, V. E. (1970). *Human sexual inadequacy.* Boston: Little, Brown.

Matsakis, A. (1998). *Managing client anger.* Oakland, CA: New Harbinger.

Maultsby, M. (1971). Systematic written homework in psychotherapy. *Rational Living, 6,* 16–23.

Maupin, E. W. (1965). Individual differences in response to a Zen meditation exercise. *Journal of Consulting Psychology, 29,* 139–145.

Maupin, E. W. (1972). On meditation. In C. Tart (Ed.), *Altered states of consciousness.* New York: Doubleday.

Mazzuca, S. A. (1982). Does patient education in chronic disease have therapeutic value? *Journal of Chronic Disease, 35,* 521–529.

McCown, W. G., & Johnson, J. (1993). *Therapy with treatment resistant families.* New York: Haworth.

McHolland, J. D. (1985). Strategies for dealing with resistant adolescents. *Adolescence, 20,* 349–368.

Meichenbaum, D. (1977). *Cognitive-behavior modification: An integrated approach.* New York: Plenum.

Meichenbaum, D., & Gilmore, J. B. (1982). Resistance from a cognitive-behavioral perspective. In P. L. Wachtel (Ed.), *Resistance: Psychodynamic and behavioral approaches.* New York: Plenum.

Meichenbaum, D., & Turk, D. C. (1987). *Facilitating treatment adherence.* New York: Plenum.

Mennicke, S. A., Lent, R. W., & Burgoyne, K. L. (1988). Premature termination from university counseling centers: A review. *Journal of Counseling and Development, 66,* 458–465.

Menninger, K. A. (1973). *Theory of psychoanalytic technique* (2nd ed.). New York: Basic.

Miller, W. R., & Rollnick, S. (1991). *Motivational interviewing: Preparing people to change addictive behavior.* New York: Guilford.

Mohl, P. C., Martinez, D., Ticknor, C., Huang, M., & Cordell, L. (1991). Early dropouts from psychotherapy. *Journal of Nervous and Mental Disease, 179,* 478–481.

Morgan, R. D. (1986). *Individual differences in the occurrence of psychological reactance and therapeutic outcome.* Unpublished doctoral dissertation, University of Nebraska at Lincoln.

Morris, R. J., & Suckerman, K. (1974a). The importance of the therapeutic relationship in systematic desensitization. *Journal of Consulting and Clinical Psychology, 42,* 148.

Morris, R. J., & Suckerman, K. (1974b). Therapist warmth as a factor in automated systematic desensitization. *Journal of Consulting and Clinical Psychology, 42,* 244–250.

Munjack, D. J., & Oziel, L. J. (1978). Resistance in the behavioral treatment of sexual dysfunctions. *Journal of Sex and Marital Therapy, 4,* 122–138.

Murphy, G. E., Cramer, B., & Lillie, L. (1984). Cognitive therapy and pharmacotherapy, singly and together in the treatment of depression. *Archives of General Psychiatry, 41,* 33–41.

Murphy, K. C., & Strong, S. R. (1972). Some effects of similarity self-disclosure. *Journal of Counseling Psychology, 19,* 121–124.

Neimeyer, R. A., & Feixas, G. (1990). The role of homework and skill acquisition in the outcome of group cognitive therapy for depression. *Behavior Therapy, 21,* 281–292.

Neuman, C. F. (1994). Understanding client resistance: Methods for enhancing motivation to change. *Cognitive and Behavioral Practice, 1,* 47–69.

Nichter, M., & Trockman, G. (1983). *Toward a psychosociocultural evaluation of the psychiatric patient: Contribution from clinical anthropology.* Unpublished manuscript, Department of Psychiatry, School of Medicine, University of Hawaii at Honolulu.

Nietzel, M. T., Guthrie, P. R., & Susman, D. T. (1990). Utilization of community and social support resources. In F. H. Kanfer & A. P. Goldstein (Eds.), *Helping people change: A textbook of methods.* New York: Pergamon.

Nitsun, M. (1996). *The anti-group: Destructive forces in the group and their creative potential.* London: Routledge.

Noonan, J. R. (1973). A follow-up of pretherapy dropouts. *Journal of Community Psychology, 1,* 43–44.

Novaco, R. (1975). *Anger control: The development and evaluation of an experimental treatment.* Lexington, MA: D. C. Heath.

O'Hanlon, W. H., & Weiner-Davis, M. (1989). *In search of solutions: A new direction in psychotherapy.* New York: W. W. Norton.

O'Keefe, D. J. (1990). *Persuasion: Theory and research.* Newbury Park, CA: Sage.

Omodei, M. M., & Wearing, A. J. (1990). Need satisfaction and involvement in personal projects: Toward an integrative model of subjective well-being. *Journal of Personality and Social Psychology, 59,* 762–769.

Orlinsky, D. E., Grawe, K., & Parks, B. K. (1994). Process and outcome in psychotherapy—noch einmal. In A. E. Bergin & S. L. Garfield (Eds.), *Handbook of psychotherapy and behavior change*. New York: Wiley.

Orne, M. T., & Wender, P. H. (1968). Anticipatory socialization for psychotherapy. *American Journal of Psychiatry, 124,* 1202–1212.

Otani, A. (1989). Client resistance in counseling: Its theoretical rationale and taxonomic classification. *Journal of Counseling and Development, 67,* 458–561.

Paar, D. W. (1990). Black holes only have room for one. In J. A. Travers (Ed.), *Psychotherapy and the remote patient*. New York: Haworth.

Parry, G. (1986). Paid employment, life events, social support, and mental health in working-class matters. *Journal of Health and Social Behavior, 27,* 193–208.

Patterson, C. H. (1966). *Theories of counseling and psychotherapy*. New York: Harper and Row.

Patterson, G. R. (1982). *Coercive family process*. Eugene, OR: Castalia.

Pedersen, P. B. (1986). Developing interculturally skilled counselors: A prototype for training. In H. P. Lefley & P. B. Pedersen (Eds.), *Crosscultural training for mental health professionals*. Springfield, IL: Charles C. Thomas.

Pekarik, G. (1985). Coping with dropouts. *Professional Psychology: Research and Practice, 16,* 114–123.

Pelham, W., & Murphy, H. A. (1986). Attention deficit and conduct disorders. In M. Hersen (Ed.), *Pharmacological and behavioral treatments: An integrative approach*. New York: Wiley.

Pereira, G. J. (1978). *Teaching empathy through skill building versus interpersonal anxiety reduction methods*. Unpublished doctoral dissertation, Catholic University of America, Washington, DC.

Persons, J. B., Burns, D. D., & Perloff, J. M. (1988). Predictors of drop out and outcome in cognitive therapy for depression in a private practice setting. *Cognitive Therapy and Research, 12,* 287–300.

Pesso, A. (1969). *Movement in psychotherapy*. New York: New York University Press.

Petty, R. E., & Cacioppo, J. T. (1986). *Communication and persuasion: Central and peripheral routes to attitude change*. New York: Springer-Verlag.

Petty, R. E., & Wegener, D. T. (1998). Attitude change: Multiple roles for persuasion variables. In D. T. Gilbert, S. T. Fiske, & G. Lindzey (Eds.), *The handbook of social psychology* (2nd ed.). New York: McGraw-Hill.

Phillips, E. L., & Fagan, P. J. (1982, August). *Attrition: Focus on the intake and first therapy interviews*. Paper presented at the annual meeting of the American Psychological Association, Washington, DC.

Pipes, R. B., & Davenport, D. S. (1990). *Introduction to psychotherapy*. Englewood Cliffs, NJ: Prentice Hall.

Primakoff, L., Epstein, N., & Covi, L. (1986). Homework compliance: An uncontrolled variable in cognitive therapy outcome research. *Behavior Therapy, 17,* 433–446.

Prochaska, J. O., DiClemente, C. C., & Norcross, J. C. (1992). In search of how people change: Applications to addictive behaviors. *American Psychologist, 47,* 1102–1114.

Prochaska, J. O., Wilcox, N., & Rossi, J. S. (1988). *Change processes used within and between therapy sessions related to outcome in a small N longitudinal study.* Unpublished manuscript, Department of Psychology, University of Rhode Island at Kingston.

Rabavilas, R., Boulougouris, J. C., & Perissaki, C. (1979). Therapist qualities related to outcome with exposure in vivo in neurotic patients. *Journal of Behavior Therapy and Experimental Psychiatry, 10,* 293–299.

Rank, O. (1945). *Will therapy and truth and reality.* New York: Knopf.

Rappaport, R. L. (1997). *Motivating clients in therapy: Values, love, and the real relationship.* London: Routledge.

Rausch, H. L., & Bordin, E. S. (1957). Warmth in personality development and in psychotherapy. *Psychiatry, 20,* 351–363.

Redl, R., & Wineman, D. (1957). *The aggressive child.* Glencoe, IL: Free Press.

Reich, W. (1951). *Character analysis* (3rd ed.; T. P. Wolfe, Trans.). New York: Farrar, Straus and Giroux. (Original work published 1933)

Reik, T. (1949). *Listening with the third ear.* New York: Farrar, Straus and Giroux.

Reis, B. F., & Brown, L. G. (1999). Reducing psychotherapy dropouts: Maximizing convergence in the psychotherapy dyad. *Psychotherapy, 36,* 123–136.

Robbins, J. M., Beck, P. R., Mueller, D. P., & Mizener, D. A. (1988). Therapists' perceptions of difficult patients. *Journal of Nervous and Mental Disorders, 176,* 490–497.

Robertson, M. H. (1988). Assessing and intervening in client motivation for psychotherapy. *Journal of Integrative and Eclectic Psychotherapy, 7,* 319–329.

Rocks, T. G., Baker, S. B., & Guerney, B. G. (1982). *Effects of counselor-directed relationship enhancement training on underachieving, poorly communicating students and their teachers.* Unpublished manuscript, Pennsylvania State University.

Rogers, C. R. (1957). The necessary and sufficient conditions of therapeutic personality change. *Journal of Counseling Psychology, 21,* 95–103.

Rogers, C. R. (1961). *On becoming a person.* Boston: Houghton Mifflin.

Rolf, I. (1977). *Rolfing: The integration of human structures.* Boulder, CO: The Rolf Institute.

Rook, K. S., & Dooley, D. (1985). Applying social support research: Theoretical problems and future directions. *Journal of Social Issues, 41,* 5–28.

Rosenthal, R. (1966). *Experimenter effects in behavioral research.* New York: Appleton-Century-Crofts.

Rosenthal, R., & DePaulo, B. M. (Eds.). (1979). *Skills in nonverbal communication.* Cambridge, MA: Oelgeschlager, Gunn, and Hain.

Rosenthal, T. L., & Steffek, B. D. (1991). Modeling methods. In F. H. Kanfer & A. P. Goldstein (Eds.), *Helping people change*. New York: Pergamon.

Rounsaville, B. J., Dolinsky, Z. S., Babor, T. F., & Meyer, R. E. (1987). Psychopathology as a predictor of treatment in alcoholics. *Archives of General Psychiatry, 44*, 505–513.

Ryle, A. (1994). Consciousness and psychotherapy. *British Journal of Medical Psychology, 67*, 115–123.

Sabalis, R. F. (1969). *Subject authoritarianism, interviewer status, and interpersonal attraction*. Unpublished master's thesis, Syracuse University.

Sackett, D. L., & Haynes, R. B. (Eds.). (1976). *Compliance with therapeutic regimens*. Baltimore: Johns Hopkins University Press.

Safran, J. D., & Muran, J. C. (2000). *Negotiating the therapeutic alliance*. New York: Guilford.

Safran, J. D., Muran, J. C., & Samstag, L. W. (1994). Resolving therapeutic alliance ruptures: A task analytic investigation. In A. O. Horvath & L. S. Greenberg (Eds.), *The working alliance: Theory, research, and practice*. New York: Wiley.

Safran, J. D., & Segal, Z. (1996). *Interpersonal process in cognitive therapy*. Northvale, NJ: Jason Aronson.

Salter, A. (1949). *Conditional reflex therapy*. New York: Straus and Young.

Sandler, I. N., Miller, P., Short, J., & Wolchik, S. A. (1989). Social support as a protective factor for children in stress. In D. Belle (Ed.), *Children's social networks and social supports*. New York: Wiley.

Schefft, B. K., & Kanfer, F. H. (1987). The utility of a process model in therapy: A comparative study of treatment effects. *Behavior Therapy, 18*, 113–134.

Schloss, P. J., & Smith, M. A. (1998). *Applied behavior analysis in the classroom*. Boston: Allyn and Bacon.

Schmidt, L. D., & Strong, S. R. (1970). Expert and inexpert counselors. *Journal of Counseling Psychology, 17*, 115–118.

Schneider, J. A., & Agras, W. S. (1985). A cognitive behavioral group treatment of bulimia. *British Journal of Psychiatry, 146*, 66–69.

Schneider, V., & Marren-Bell, U. (1995). Violence in the accident and emergency department. *Accident and Emergency Nursing, 3*, 74–78.

Schoenewolf, G. (1993). *Counterresistance: The therapist's interference with the therapeutic process*. Northvale, NJ: Jason Aronson.

Schuller, R., Crits-Christoph, P., & Connolly, M. B. (1991). The Resistance Scale: Background and psychometric properties. *Psychoanalytic Psychology, 8*, 195–211.

Schulman, B. A. (1979). Active patient orientation and outcomes in hypertensive treatment. *Medical Care, 17*, 267–280.

Schwartzer, R., & Fuchs, R. (1995). Changing risk behaviors and adopting health behaviors: The role of self-efficacy beliefs. In A. Bandura (Ed.), *Self-efficacy in changing societies*. Cambridge, England: Cambridge University Press.

Schwitzgebel, R. (1961). *Streetcorner research: An experimental approach to the juvenile delinquent*. Cambridge, MA: Harvard University Press.

Searles, H. (1977). *Countertransference and related subjects*. New York: International Universities Press.

Sechrest, L. B., & Strowig, R. W. (1962). Teaching machines and the individual learner. *Educational Theory, 12,* 157–169.

Seibel, C. A., & Dowd, E. T. (1999). Reactance and therapeutic noncompliance. *Cognitive Therapy and Research, 23,* 373–379.

Selekman, M. D. (1993). *Pathways to change*. New York: Guilford.

Seltzer, A., & Hoffman, B. F. (1980). Drug compliance of the psychiatric patient. *Canadian Family Physician, 26,* 725–727.

Selver, C. (1957). Sensory awareness and total functioning. *General Semantics Bulletin, 20/21,* 5–17.

Selvini-Palazzoli, M., Cecchin, M., Prata, G., & Boscolo, L. (1978). *Paradox and counterparadox*. New York: Jason Aronson.

Seibel, C. A., & & Dowd, E. T. (1999). Reactance and therapeutic compliance. *Cognitive Therapy and Research, 23,* 373–379.

Shelton, J. L. (1973). Murder strikes and panic follows—Can behavioral modification help? *Behavior Therapy, 4,* 706–708.

Shelton, J. L. (1979). Instigation therapy: Using therapeutic homework to promote treatment gains. In A. P. Goldstein & F. H. Kanfer (Eds.), *Maximizing treatment gains: Transfer enhancement in psychotherapy*. New York: Academic.

Shelton, J. L., & Levy, R. L. (1981). *Behavioral assignments and treatment compliance*. Champaign, IL: Research Press.

Shoben, E. J. (1953). Some observations on psychotherapy and the learning process. In O. H. Mowrer (Ed.), *Psychotherapy, theory and research*. New York: Ronald Press.

Shoham-Salomon, V., & Rosenthal, R. (1987). Paradoxical interventions: A meta-analysis. *Journal of Counseling and Clinical Psychology, 55,* 22–28.

Shumaker, S. A., & Brownell, A. (1984). Toward a theory of social support: Closing conceptual gaps. *Journal of Social Issues, 40,* 11–36.

Simonson, N. R. (1968). *The impact of warm and cold self-disclosing therapists*. Unpublished manuscript, Syracuse University.

Sitharthan, T., & Kavanagh, D. J. (1990). Role of self-efficacy in predicting outcomes from a programme for controlled drinking. *Drug and Alcohol Dependence, 27,* 87–94.

Slack, C. W. (1960). Experimenter-subject psychotherapy: A new method of introducing intensive office treatment for unreachable cases. *Mental Hygiene, 44,* 238–256.

Sloane, R. B. (1975). *Psychotherapy versus behavior therapy*. Cambridge, MA: Harvard University Press.

Smith, H. C. (1966). *Sensitivity to people*. New York: McGraw-Hill.

Smith, H. C. (1973). *Sensitivity training*. New York: McGraw-Hill.

Soloff, P. (1987). Emergency management of violent patients. In R. Hales & A. Frances (Eds.), *Psychiatric update: American Psychiatric Association annual review*. Washington, DC: American Psychiatric Association.

Solomon, M. A. (1974). Resistance in family therapy: Conceptual and technical considerations. *The Family Coordinator, 23*, 159–163.

Sommers-Flanagan, J., & Sommers-Flanagan, R. (1997). *Tough kids, cool counseling*. Alexandria, VA: American Counseling Association.

Spiegel, B. (1976). Expertness, similarity, and perceived counselor competence. *Journal of Counseling Psychology, 23*, 436–441.

Spotnitz, H. (1969). *Modern psychoanalysis of the schizophrenic patient*. New York: Grune and Stratton.

Steckel, S., & Swain, M. (1977). The use of written contracts to increase adherence. *Hospitals, 5*, 81–84.

Stern, E. M. (1990). The move toward responsibility: Psychotherapy and the abrasive patient. In E. M. Stern (Ed.), *Psychotherapy and the abrasive patient*. New York: Haworth.

Stimson, G. V. (1974). Obeying doctor's orders: A view from the other side. *Social Science and Medicine, 8*, 97–104.

Stollak, G. E., & Guerney, B., Jr. (1964). Exploration of personal problems by juvenile delinquents under conditions of minimal reinforcement. *Journal of Clinical Psychology, 20*, 279–283.

Stoltenberg, C. D., Leach, M. M., & Bratt, A. (1989). The elaboration likelihood model and psychotherapeutic persuasion. *Journal of Cognitive Psychotherapy, 3*, 181–199.

Stone, G. C. (1979). Patient compliance and the role of the expert. *Journal of Social Issues, 35*, 34–59.

Storch, R. R., & Lane, R. C. (1989). Resistance in mandated psychotherapy: Its function and management. *Journal of Contemporary Psychotherapy, 19*, 25–38.

Strean, H. S. (1985). *Resolving resistances in psychotherapy*. New York: Wiley.

Strean, H. S. (1995). *Resolving counter-resistances in psychotherapy*. New York: Brunner/Mazel.

Strong, S. R. (1968). Counseling: An interpersonal influence process. *Journal of Counseling Psychology, 15*, 215–224.

Strong, S. R. (1978). Social psychological approach to psychotherapy research. In A. E. Bergin & S. L. Garfield (Eds.), *Handbook of psychotherapy and behavior change*. New York: Wiley.

Strong, S. R., & Schmidt, L. D. (1970). Expertnesss and influence in counseling. *Journal of Counseling Psychology, 17*, 81–87.

Strupp, H. H., & Bloxom, A. L. (1973). Preparing lower-class patients for group psychotherapy: Development and evaluation of a role induction film. *Journal of Consulting and Clinical Psychology, 41*, 373–384.

Sue, D. W., & Sue, D. (1999). *Counseling the culturally different*. New York: Wiley.

Sue, S. (1988). Psychotherapeutic services for ethnic minorities: Two decades of research findings. *American Psychologist, 43*, 301–308.

Sundel, M. (1982). *Behavior modification in the human services*. Englewood Cliffs, NJ: Prentice Hall.

Tageson, C. W. (1982). *Humanistic psychology: A synthesis*. Homewood, IL: Dorsey.

Tasca, G. A., & McMullen, L. M. (1992). Interpersonal complementarity and antitheses within a stage model of psychotherapy. *Psychotherapy: Theory, Research, and Practice, 29*, 515–523.

Taylor, G. J. (1984). Psychotherapy with the boring patient. *Canadian Journal of Psychiatry, 29*, 515–222.

Tennen, H., Rohrbaugh, M., Press, S., & White, L. (1981). Reactance theory and therapeutic paradox: A compliance-defiance model. *Psychotherapy: Theory, Research and Practice, 18*, 14–23.

Teyber, E. (1988). *Interpersonal process in psychotherapy*. Chicago: Dorsey.

Travers, J. A. (Ed.). (1990). *Psychotherapy and the remote patient*. New York: Haworth.

Truax, C. B., & Carkhuff, R. R. (1967). *Toward effective counseling and psychotherapy*. Chicago: Aldine.

Vaux, A. (1988). *Social support*. New York: Praeger.

Verhulst, J. C., & van de Vijver, F. J. R. (1990). Resistance during psychotherapy and behavior therapy. *Behavior Modification, 14* , 172–187.

Wachtel, P. L. (1980). What should we say to our patients? On the wording of therapists' comments. *Psychotherapy: Theory, Research and Practice, 17*, 183–188.

Wachtel, P. L. (1982). Introduction: Resistance and the process of therapeutic change. In P. L. Wachtel (Ed.), *Resistance: Psychodynamic and behavioral approaches*. New York: Plenum.

Wade, P., & Berstein, B. (1991). Culture sensitivity training and counselor's race: Effects on Black female clients' perceptions and attrition. *Journal of Counseling Psychology, 38*, 9–15.

Walsh, W. G. (1971). *The effects of conformity pressure and modeling on the attraction of hospitalized patients toward an interviewer*. Unpublished doctoral dissertation, Syracuse University.

Ward, D. A., & Allivise, K. J. (1979). Effects of legal coercion in the treatment of alcohol related criminal offenders. *Justice System Journal, 5*, 107–111.

Ward, T., & Hudson, S. M. (1998). A model of the relapse process in sexual offenders. *Journal of Interpersonal Violence, 13*, 700–725.

Wathney, S. (1982). Paradoxical interventions in transactional analysis and Gestalt therapy. *Transactional Analysis Journal, 12*, 185–189.

Weeks, G. R., & L'Abate, L. (1982). *Paradoxical psychotherapy: Theory and practice with individuals, couples and families.* New York: Brunner/Mazel.

Weighill, V. E., Hodge, J., & Peck, D. F. (1983). Keeping appointments with clinical psychologists. *British Journal of Clinical Psychology, 22,* 143–144.

Weinberg, N. H., & Zaslove, M. (1963). "Resistance" to systematic desensitization of phobias. *Journal of Clinical Psychology, 19,* 179–181.

Weiss, J., & Sampson, H. (1986). *The psychoanalytic process: Theory, clinical observations, and empirical research.* New York: Guilford.

Weiss, R. S. (1974). The provisions of social relations. In Z. Rubin (Ed.), *Doing unto others.* Englewood Cliffs, NJ: Prentice Hall.

Wepman, B. J., & Donovan, M. W. (1984). Abrasiveness: Description and dynamic issues. In E. M. Stern (Ed.), *Psychotherapy and the abrasive patient.* New York: Haworth.

Williams, K. E., & Chambless, D. L. (1990). The relationship between therapist characteristics and outcome of in vivo exposure treatment for agoraphobia. *Behavior Therapy, 21,* 111–116.

Williams, S. L. (1995). Self-efficacy and anxiety and phobic disorders. In J. E. Maddux (Ed.), *Self-efficacy, adaptation, and adjustment: Theory, research, and application.* New York: Plenum.

Willis, R. J. (1984). The many faces of the hesitant patient. In J. A. Travers (Ed.), *Psychotherapy and the uncommitted patient.* New York: Haworth.

Willis, T. A. (1982). *Basic processes in helping relationships.* New York: Academic.

Wissler, A. L. (1990). Romancing remoteness in psychotherapy. In J. A. Travers (Ed.), *Psychotherapy and the remote patient.* New York: Haworth.

Wong, N. (1983). Perspectives on the difficult patient. *Bulletin of the Menninger Clinic, 47,* 99–106.

Yalom, I. D. (1970). *The theory and practice of group psychotherapy.* New York: Basic.

Yalom, I. D., Houts, P. S., Newell, G., & Rand, K. H. (1967). Preparation of patients for group therapy. *Archives of General Psychiatry, 17,* 416–427.

Yalom, I. D., & Lieberman, M. A. (1971). A study of encounter group casualties. *Archives of General Psychiatry, 25,* 16–30.

Zettle, R. D., & Hayes, S. C. (1987). Component and process analysis of cognitive therapy. *Psychological Reports, 61,* 929–953.

Name Index

Subject Index

Note: Tables are indicated by an italicized *t* following the page number.

About the Author

Arnold P. Goldstein joined the clinical psychology section of Syracuse University's Psychology Department in 1963 and both taught there and directed its Psychotherapy Center until 1980. In 1981, he founded the university's Center for Research on Aggression. He joined Syracuse University's Division of Special Education in 1985 and in 1990 helped organize and codirect the New York State Taskforce on Juvenile Gangs. Dr. Goldstein has a career-long interest, as both researcher and practitioner, in difficult-to-reach clients. Since 1980, his main research and psycho-educational focus has been youth violence. Dr. Goldstein's many books include, among others, *Delinquents on Delinquency; The Gang Intervention Handbook;* and the recently revised editions of *Skillstreaming the Adolescent: New Strategies and Perspectives for Teaching Prosocial Skills; Aggression Replacement Training: A Comprehensive Intervention for Aggressive Youth;* and *The Prepare Curriculum: Teaching Prosocial Competencies.* The present volume focuses on ways to motivate clients to initiate and stay with the therapeutic process. A companion to this one, his recent book *Lasting Change: Methods for Enhancing Generalization of Gain* looks at ways to promote transfer and maintenance once therapy is over.